How to Beat

Panic

Also in the series

How to Beat Agoraphobia
Pamela Myles-Hooton

How to Beat Fears and Phobias
Mark Papworth

How to Beat Insomnia and Sleep Problems
Kirstie Anderson

How to Beat Depression and Persistent Low Mood
Mark Papworth

How to Beat Worry
Liz Kell

PAMELA MYLES-HOOTON

How to Beat
Panic

A Brief, Evidence-based
Self-help Treatment

ROBINSON

ROBINSON

First published in Great Britain in 2026 by Robinson

1 3 5 7 9 10 8 6 4 2

Copyright © Pamela Myles-Hooton, 2026
Illustrations by Liane Payne

The moral right of the author has been asserted.

Important Note
This book is not intended as a substitute for medical advice
or treatment. Any person with a condition requiring medical
attention should consult a qualified medical practitioner
or suitable therapist.

All rights reserved.
No part of this publication may be reproduced, stored in a retrieval
system, or transmitted, in any form, or by any means, without
the prior permission in writing of the publisher, nor be otherwise
circulated in any form of binding or cover other than that in which
it is published and without a similar condition including this
condition being imposed on the subsequent purchaser.

A CIP catalogue record for this book
is available from the British Library.

ISBN: 978-1-47214-873-5

Typeset in Minion by Initial Typesetting Services, Edinburgh
Printed and bound in Great Britain by Clays Ltd, Elcograf S.p.A.

Papers used by Robinson are from well-managed forests
and other responsible sources.

Robinson	The authorised representative
An imprint of	in the EEA is
Little, Brown Book Group	Hachette Ireland,
Carmelite House	8 Castlecourt Centre,
50 Victoria Embankment	Dublin 15, D15 XTP3, Ireland
London EC4Y 0DZ	(email: info@hbgi.ie)

An Hachette UK Company
www.hachette.co.uk

www.littlebrown.co.uk

CONTENTS

Section 1: Getting going	1
Section 2: Understanding panic disorder	47
Section 3: Strategies to overcome panic disorder	89
Section 4: The relapse management toolkit	159
Section 5: Recovery stories	181
Workbook	197
Further resources	233
Acknowledgements	241
Index	243

Section 1

GETTING GOING

Well done for making the first step!

Hello! Often, it's the first step that's the hardest. By starting to read this book you have taken not only the first but one of the most important steps on your road to recovery from panic disorder. You may have been living with panic disorder for many years, or you may have just recently started experiencing panic attacks and are concerned that they won't simply go away. You may be frightened by the experience. This is natural and understandable. Panic attacks can severely restrict your ability to get on with what you want to do in life.

Often, in order to get better, we first have to reach a point where we are willing to invest time and energy into the task of addressing the problem. This is because psychological approaches usually involve a great deal of personal effort. This is needed to reap the full benefits of what they have to offer. So, before we start, do please think about whether you have this time and effort available. Sometimes this is not exactly the right time for action but the fact you are reading this book now is a sign that you are getting ready to do something about it. We'll return to this later in this section.

The strategies in this book are based on the principles of cognitive behavioural therapy (CBT), an evidence-based psychological approach that has been shown to help people with this type of problem. These strategies have been used by mental health professionals to help people to overcome their panic disorder (one of the most common of several anxiety disorders). They have been tried, tested, refined, and have helped millions of people beat their panic disorder.

About me

First, I should introduce myself and explain why I have written this book. I am author/co-author of several educational texts, academic publications and self-help books including *The CBT Handbook*, *How to Beat Agoraphobia* and *Living Well with Type 2 Diabetes*. For over twenty years I was an accredited cognitive behavioural therapist, during which time I mainly worked in the NHS. Overlapping with this work, I spent over eleven years training others in delivering evidence-based psychological interventions for people with common mental health problems (including panic disorder) at the University of Reading.

More recently I have worked with NHS Education for Scotland to develop a training programme for mental health staff who help people experiencing panic disorder as well as other common mental health conditions. In 2021, I became one of three founding directors of a company which operates as a not-for-profit for the NHS and charities, providing online training for mental health professionals in evidence-based psychological treatments. I also sit on the NHS Expert Advisory Group for Talking Therapies for Anxiety and Depression. Outside of work I enjoy interrailing, attending live comedy and music gigs as well as cooking for friends.

What you will find in this section

In this section, we will look at the terms commonly referred to throughout this book, and explain the difference between isolated panic attacks, panic disorder and agoraphobia as well as other circumstances where panic attacks are likely to happen. We will then look at how CBT self-help can work for you including some top tips on how to get the most out of this book. I also provide a brief summary of the other sections of the book and encourage you to give it a go! We will end the section on setting goals for what you want to achieve by using this book.

Frequently used terms

Panic: a sudden extreme feeling of anxiety or fear.

Anxiety: a feeling of unease, such as worry or fear, which can be mild, moderate or severe.

Fear: an unpleasant, and often strong, emotion caused by the anticipation, threat or awareness of danger.

Apprehension: a sense of foreboding and worry about the future, or a fear that something unpleasant is going to happen.

Understanding panic disorder and its related conditions

Panic attacks, panic disorder and agoraphobia

This is a good time to define panic attacks, panic disorder and its common companion, agoraphobia, before moving onto other problems where panic attacks can happen.

What is a panic attack?

Panic attacks are very common – research shows that up to 28% of the general population will experience them occasionally and unexpectedly at some point in their lives. A panic attack is a brief episode of sudden and very intense anxiety/fear/apprehension which commonly peaks within five to ten minutes and usually lasts fifteen to twenty minutes but can last up to thirty. Some of the common symptoms that people experience during a panic attack include: heart racing; sweating; dry mouth; chest pain; light-headedness; a fear that something catastrophic is about to happen like a heart attack or even being about to die; and other symptoms we will go into detail about later. *Although these symptoms can be extremely frightening, they are not dangerous!*

'Sometimes I panic for hours – what then?'

It is not possible to have a panic attack for that long. Symptoms that last for much longer than thirty minutes, say hours, are *anxiety* rather than *panic*. This is an important distinction. *That is not to be dismissive of anxiety, it is bad enough, but it is not the same as the intense sensations of a panic attack.*

What is panic disorder?

Panic disorder is an anxiety disorder in which the person regularly has panic attacks. It is estimated that 4% of the global population currently have an anxiety disorder, making anxiety the most common of all mental health disorders. Three to five per cent of the population will experience panic disorder at some point in their lifetime. It is the most common anxiety disorder that people seek help for. It is twice as common in women as it is in men and tends to start in early adulthood (the mid-twenties).

Anxiety and panic attacks are completely normal, and anxiety can be appropriate in some stressful or dangerous situations, so it is a useful emotion to have. For instance, it would be considered normal to feel anxious before taking an exam. If we are in a dangerous situation, a degree of anxiety will trigger action to make ourselves safe. But, when a person has panic disorder, they will regularly experience panic and anxiety in non-dangerous, everyday situations such as being alone at home, in a busy shop or using public transport. Panic can also appear as if it has *come out of the blue*. This can be extremely distressing and lead the person to live in a cycle of *fear of fear*, avoiding the places where panic tends to happen. This can result in further problems such as agoraphobia – *around one in three people with panic disorder go on to develop agoraphobia.*

Do I have panic disorder?

To be formally diagnosed with panic disorder, you will experience recurrent and unexpected panic attacks and some accompanying symptoms from the following list:

Common panic disorder symptoms

- Palpitations, heart pounding/racing
- Sweating
- Trembling or shaking
- Shortness of breath or the feeling of being smothered
- Choking sensations
- Chest pain
- Nausea
- Tummy upset or discomfort
- Dizziness, light-headedness, feeling unsteady or faint
- Chills or heat sensations
- Numbness or tingling
- Feelings of unreality or like you are detached from yourself

- Fear of losing control or 'going mad'
- Fear that you are going to die

This list of common symptoms of panic disorder can be found in Worksheet 1, where you can tick those that apply to you.

Here are some examples of how people describe what a panic attack feels like:

'It's as if I am being crushed by a vice.'

'I freeze and can't move, it feels like I'm going to die.'

'I think I'm having a heart attack.'

'I feel like I'm dying and going mad at the same time.'

Symptoms of panic attacks and fear of their consequences

Believing you are about to experience a major physical event such as a heart attack, fainting episode or loss of sanity is extremely frightening. Perhaps it is not surprising that people with panic disorder experiencing the symptoms associated with these fears can end up in an Accident and Emergency department. When medical tests are conducted by healthcare professionals, generally nothing untoward is found in the test results.

We will come on to key differences between symptoms of heart attacks, fainting, and going insane versus panic attacks in Section 3. *What is key here is that someone has interpreted their symptoms as dangerous, but such thoughts are not always correct.* We will explore the role of thoughts and how they influence the severity of panic attacks in Section 2.

Panic disorder symptom scale (PDSS)

This questionnaire has proven to be an excellent tool for measuring panic disorder symptom severity. It includes seven questions about common panic symptoms and how much the person has been affected by them over the last week. The range of overall scores is 0–28. A total score of 8 or above can indicate a person has panic disorder. However, this is not a diagnostic tool, rather it can be a helpful way to measure progress when tackling panic symptoms. A person without panic disorder could score highly for a week if they were having a stressful time (e.g. if they had several college exams or interviews over the week) which would understandably elevate scores. If you score less than 8 but are troubled by panic symptoms you are still likely to benefit from this book. You can find the PDSS on lots of websites (including www.onlinecbtresources.co.uk/panic-disorder-severity-scale where you can complete it online) or you can print it from www.goodmedicine.org.uk/goodknowledge/panic-ocd-depersonalization-information-assessment. Now is a good time to complete this questionnaire. You should try to complete this scale weekly as you work through the book. Each time you complete the PDSS, plot your scores on the graph in Worksheet 2.

What is agoraphobia?

Agoraphobia is an anxiety disorder in which the person has a fear of being in situations where they believe that escape may be difficult or that help will not be available if something goes wrong. Agoraphobia can develop as a complication to panic disorder (this is very common) as the person associates panic attacks with places where they have previously occurred. This leads to *avoidance*. In agoraphobia, it is not uncommon for people to experience difficulty using public transport, standing in a queue, being in a crowd, being away from home alone or being in enclosed spaces where exiting may be difficult such as shops, theatres or cinemas.

In addition to the catastrophic fears that are a key feature of panic disorder (e.g., collapsing, having a heart attack, going insane), people often describe additional fears of the *social consequences* of their panic attacks (e.g., making a fool of themselves). Not all agoraphobia is related to panic attacks. It may be down to, for example, fear of crime, accident or illness. *When we talk about agoraphobia in this book it will always be in the context of panic disorder with agoraphobia.*

Do I have agoraphobia too?

As mentioned, many people with panic disorder go on to develop agoraphobia too. This is because a person may associate panic attacks with places or situations where panic attacks have happened repeatedly. The person may develop a fear that panic attacks or other incapacitating or embarrassing symptoms will occur in a number of situations. As a result, they may actively avoid these situations, need to have someone with them, or endure them with intense fear or anxiety.

Common agoraphobia symptoms

To be formally diagnosed with agoraphobia, you will experience marked fear or anxiety about two or more of the following five 'problem areas' for at least several months:

- Transport:
    - Being a passenger in a taxi
    - Using the bus or tram
    - Travelling by train
    - Using the underground
    - Sailing on ships
    - Travelling by aeroplane
- Open spaces:
    - Car parks
    - Marketplaces
- Enclosed spaces:
    - Shops
    - Supermarkets
    - Department stores
    - Theatres
    - Cinemas
- Standing in a queue

- Being in a crowd
- Being away from home alone

This list of common symptoms of agoraphobia can be found in Worksheet 3 where you can tick those that apply to you. It may be that some of these situations are relatively easy to tackle if you are accompanied, but seem much more difficult or impossible to do on your own. Provide ticks when thinking about doing each one alone. It may be that you have panic disorder with agoraphobia. This is common and does not affect your chances of beating them both.

As mentioned, agoraphobia can be a problem in its own right (not secondary to panic attacks). If that is the case for you, I would direct you to another book in this series, *How to Beat Agoraphobia*. If you have panic disorder *with* agoraphobia, please stick with this book, as it is designed with you in mind.

Understanding panic disorder

Having panic disorder means that you can experience or worry about having the symptoms of panic attacks, their unpredictable nature (*coming out of the blue*), and where they might occur (often when away from home or when home alone). This panic and fear of panic attacks is likely to affect your daily routine and can at times feel like it is severely limiting your life. It is like being locked in a psychological cage and sometimes it can affect those around you too. You might have tried to overcome your panic attacks before but not succeeded. It can be a difficult thing to do. Loved ones may have offered well-meaning advice which might not have helped, despite your best efforts to follow it. It can be hard to know how or where to start. For this reason, this book is written in several sections that will allow you to address your panic disorder at a pace that is manageable for you. It will do so in a way that should allow you to beat your panic attacks and begin living your life to the full.

There are several other topics relevant to the experience and treatment of panic disorder that I wish to cover before talking about how the book is structured and how it might be best used:

- Use of medication
- How panic disorder is different from other disorders with some similar symptoms
- The causes of panic disorder
- What is cognitive behavioural therapy (CBT)?
- Using CBT self-help

Medication for panic disorder

If your panic disorder is longstanding or you have not benefited from self-help or psychological therapy such as CBT, you may wish to speak to your doctor about the possibility of trying a pharmacological intervention. In the 1960s, it was not uncommon for people with anxiety and panic disorder to be prescribed a benzodiazepine (the varieties of this medication generally end with the letters 'pam', for instance diazepam and lorazepam). Nowadays, these medications would not be prescribed due to their addictive nature. Rather, several antidepressants have been found to be helpful in the treatment of panic disorder. Your doctor will know which these are and whether they are likely to be appropriate for you. However, I would recommend that you try a CBT intervention first, such as the one covered in this book.

How is panic disorder different to other anxiety disorders?

We defined panic disorder on page 6. Panic disorder is different to a normal fear reaction because the person will experience:

- frequent unexpected panic attacks (apparently coming out of the blue);

- persistent worry or concern about future panic attacks ('I fear when I will have the next one') or their implications ('there must be something wrong with me');

- and changes in behaviour such as avoiding certain activities or places in an attempt to prevent panic attacks from recurring, which can result in a significant impairment to day-to-day functioning.

Panic attacks do not only happen in panic disorder. Here are some other anxiety disorders that might be confused with panic disorder. Your doctor will be able to help you determine which issue you are experiencing (if any) if you are unclear about this:

- *Social anxiety disorder.* This is anxiety about speaking in front of others where the person fears that they may be judged negatively in some way (this can range from giving a speech at a wedding to speaking casually in groups or with a stranger). The person is concerned they will act in a way or show anxiety symptoms that will mean others see them in a negative light. People can experience panic attacks in these situations.

- *Post-traumatic stress disorder (PTSD).* Here panic attacks are triggered by memories following the experience of an extremely threatening or horrific event or series of events. It is characterised by re-experiencing symptoms such as flashbacks (involuntary memories that make a person feel like they are reliving the traumatic event) and/or nightmares; avoidance of thoughts, memories, and/or reminders of the event; and persistent feelings of heightened threat (e.g., jumping when hearing a loud noise).

- *Specific phobia.* People with specific phobias will experience excessive fear or anxiety when faced with, or when they think that they are going to be faced with, objects or situations such as certain animals, heights or enclosed spaces. The person may have a panic attack in these circumstances. Agoraphobia is not considered a specific phobia due to the fear and anxiety occurring in response to a group of situations where escape might be difficult, or help might not be available, as described earlier.

- *Generalised anxiety disorder (GAD).* Although people with GAD can also experience panic attacks, they are more worried and preoccupied by a number of everyday events rather than panic attacks or the consequences of them. GAD is characterised by fear that generally something bad may happen and/or excessive worry focused on a variety of areas such as family, health, finances or work. This fear is often accompanied by symptoms of muscular tension or restlessness.

- *Depression.* People who are depressed may feel panicky, especially in the morning. If the person was not having panic attacks prior to becoming depressed, it is likely that the panic attacks are part of their depression. In this case, treatment of the depression is the priority. If the person was having panic attacks prior to the depression, the depression may be a secondary problem and may lift when panic symptoms improve.

Causes of panic disorder

As with many psychological problems, the exact cause of panic disorder is not fully known, and working hard to find the cause is unlikely to take the problem away. We know that isolated and occasional panic attacks are common. It would therefore be difficult to find one single reason for the cause of a panic disorder. It is more likely that there are numerous reasons. Stressful life events including relationship break-ups, loss of a loved one, illness, higher than usual caffeine consumption, drugs, or hormonal changes could all be in the frame for causing changes to body sensations that lead to the occasional panic attack.

Yet not everyone goes on to develop panic disorder after such events – why? According to our understanding in CBT, the people that go on to develop panic disorder will interpret their body sensations in a catastrophic way (e.g., *these palpitations must mean there is something wrong with my heart*). Later we will look back at the first panic attack that triggered your panic disorder to see whether this is the case for you.

As we know, many people with panic disorder will develop agoraphobia to some extent. Agoraphobia seems to be more likely to occur if the early panic attacks take place outside the home when the person is alone in situations where getting away might be difficult or help might be harder to access. People who have panic disorder without any agoraphobic avoidance are more likely to have had their first panic attacks when they were at home without other people around.

Making sense of your first panic attack which progressed to panic disorder can be useful – and most people remember their first panic attack like it happened yesterday! You may be able to look back at your first panic attack and make sense of why it happened, or it may seem like it came out of the blue; this is very common. It can often be useful to track the journey of your panic attacks and distinguish between your first and the progression to repeated panic attacks and development of panic disorder (we will use a diary for tracking your panic attacks a little later).

What is cognitive behavioural therapy (CBT)?

This book is based on an evidence-based psychological approach called cognitive behavioural therapy, or CBT for short. The evidence supporting this approach comes from many research trials which are summarised into important scientific reviews. These reviews say that CBT is effective for many people who experience anxiety difficulties including panic disorder and agoraphobia. Of course, sometimes people with an anxiety disorder will also become depressed due to the consequences of experiencing long-term anxiety and this is common in panic disorder. CBT can be useful when this is the case too.

CBT can be provided in a number of ways including:

- with a therapist in person;
- by telephone or using online technology;

- in a group setting with others also living with panic disorder;
- or in a self-help format such as provided by this book.

Sometimes you can get support while using self-help from a healthcare professional. A family member or friend can also act as a supporter. I talk about this more later in this section.

Using CBT self-help

One of the advantages of self-help is that you can use the tools described within the book at a pace that best suits you. In saying that, like taking a course of medicine, the approach works best if you keep going with it consistently rather than trying it for a while, having a rest for a month then picking it up again. Like a course of many prescription medications, self-help works best if you engage with it every day. Self-help is also an empowering approach in that you will know that the benefits you have gained have been through your own efforts.

CBT is mentioned quite often in popular media such as in magazines, newspapers and online. You might have already done some reading about panic disorder and come across CBT on the internet so you may be familiar with some of its principles. However, if this is your first experience of CBT self-help, flicking through this book may seem quite daunting. This is understandable. You may worry about what lies ahead. Try not to do so. I have done my best to make this book easy to use and have followed what I know to be best practice in writing self-help books.

How to use this book

The book is structured so that you can learn about your problem, consider goals that you want to achieve, begin to make changes, and learn how to maintain the gains you make and manage any setbacks. The book sections should allow you to pace yourself. It can be difficult to tackle this kind of problem for all sorts of reasons, especially if it has been troubling you for a long time. Do try to bear this in mind as you work your way through the exercises in the book, so that you can be forgiving of yourself when times are tough. *Remember that the benefits will repay your efforts.*

There is no right or wrong way to use this book. Some people like to read through the entire book before going back to start tackling the problem. You might prefer to work through the book in order as you go through it. You might like to read first about how the case examples (in Section 5) used CBT self-help to overcome their panic attacks to get a sense of what is expected before committing to doing it yourself. Whatever you find to be most helpful for you is absolutely fine. However, I would strongly encourage you to work through Section 2 before moving on to using the CBT strategies in Section 3.

If you are working through this book with the support of a healthcare professional, they will be able to answer any questions you might have, offer you additional advice and may even be able to help support you as needed with completing some of the exercises. If you are working through the book on your own, you are encouraged to use the worksheets and make a note of helpful bits of text or take photos of particular sections that you keep in a folder or on an electronic device. If you are not sure about something, remember that another advantage of using a self-help book is that you can simply go back and read that section or paragraph again. If you need to do this, please don't become frustrated or critical of yourself. It can feel like there is a lot to take in and *some information may contradict your current thinking*! What is most important is that you understand the strategies described within the book, not just how to do them, but the rationale for them too. So, take your time.

Sections of the book

The book is divided into five sections. There will be something in each section that is relevant to you and helps you to tackle your panic disorder. Here is an overview of what each section contains.

Section 1: Getting going

Section 1 is about getting started in working through the book. CBT self-help tends to work best if you can dedicate some time every day to tackling your problem although this may not always be possible. That is fine too but do try to dedicate up to sixty minutes, at least five times a week, more often if you can – *the more time the better!* You will have to do this for a few weeks to reap the full benefit although you may well notice some early improvements which will hopefully spur you on to keep going. *Just reading some of the content may change your thinking around your panic attacks!*

Section 2: Understanding panic disorder

In this section we'll look at what panic disorder is in more depth including triggers and what keeps it going. We'll also look at agoraphobia in more detail and how it links to panic disorder if this is the case for you. In particular, this section aims to help you understand more about how your panic attacks are impacting your life, and what may be maintaining the problem. You will also learn about the CBT panic cycle and how to apply it to your panic attacks. *Remember, panic attacks are not life-threatening even though they feel like they could be!*

Section 3: Strategies to overcome panic disorder

This section first focuses on getting a greater sense of your problem, then moves on to using CBT self-help to beat your panic disorder, and agoraphobia if relevant to you. We'll look at ways of making sense of your symptoms and how they are interlinked and consider what it is that is keeping your panic attacks going. You will be encouraged to try out a number of exercises to help you get on top of your panic disorder. There is guidance for each exercise and a diary/worksheet to use for planning, carrying out and reviewing how it went.

Section 4: The relapse management toolkit

Here the focus is on what you can do to try to ensure the changes you have made to your life are long-lasting. If your panic attacks are still significantly interfering with your life having worked through the book, we will look at what next steps you can take to address the problem. CBT self-help has been used successfully by many people to overcome panic disorder, but it is also natural to experience setbacks along the way which may lead to a re-emergence of symptoms. Life can throw all sorts of things at us that are not always expected. Therefore, we will focus on how to maintain the progress you have made and look at ways of dealing with setbacks.

Section 5: Recovery stories

In the final section, we will catch up with the case examples that are introduced in Section 2. They share their stories of having panic disorder and describe how they overcame their difficulties. You can see how they put their plans into action, what stumbling blocks they encountered along the way and how they continued to stay on top of their panic attacks. Their stories will be different to yours, but you are likely to see some similarities. The CBT strategies they used to tackle their difficulties are the same ones recommended to help you with your panic attacks.

> **Workbook**
>
> There are some written exercises and diaries that I urge you to complete – they are an important part of the treatment. You may have noticed that I referred to worksheets earlier. All the worksheets and diaries are compiled together for you at the end of the book. You can either photocopy them from the book or you print them out from overcoming.co.uk/715/resources-to-download.

Top tips on using the book

Before beginning to understand your panic attacks and how they affect you, here are some top tips about how to use this self-help book. Some of these tips apply to the use of self-help in general, not just this book. The tips come from people who have benefited from CBT self-help to overcome their difficulties and from healthcare professionals who support people in using CBT self-help.

> ### Top tip 1: Give it your best shot
>
> 'I had lived with panic attacks for ten years and didn't think there was anything that could help me. It was frightening to think of starting to go to places that I avoided because of fear of having a panic attack, especially going without my tablets in my pocket. But I gave it a go, and despite it being tough at times, I stuck with it and now I go wherever I want, and don't need to have tablets in my pocket *just in case*!'

It is unlikely that working your way through the book and trying out the CBT self-help strategies is going to be easy. There will probably be some bumps along the way. As you learn the strategies, you will need to try them out by confronting some situations that you may have been avoiding for some time. What is important is to give it your best shot and follow the guidance on how to deal with the challenges and possible setbacks that come along. Reading through the stories of others who have used these strategies to tackle their panic disorder may be helpful (see Section 5). If a healthcare professional is supporting you, talk to them about things you are finding difficult. They will be able to check that you are using the strategies in a way that is likely to bring about the most benefit as well as offer encouragement and help you to troubleshoot difficulties.

Top tip 2: Put what you have learned into action

> 'It helped me when I got an understanding of what was keeping my panic attacks going. I then took steps to tackle them head on by doing the exercises in the book. I wrote things down and recorded how I got on, which helped me learn from the changes I made and motivated me to carry on.'

This is very much a 'doing' book rather than a 'reading' book. Putting what you learn into practice is central to overcoming panic disorder. You don't need to do everything at once, but it is good to keep going without taking breaks from it – *build up momentum*. Generally speaking, the more effort you put into it, the more you will benefit. After doing some reading, putting the strategies into practice is key to addressing your panic disorder.

Think of it as being a bit like learning to drive a car. The instructor provides tuition to drive the car, and it can feel difficult to put everything that is being learned into practice at first. It is only with repeated practice that the learner becomes more confident. Without investing time putting into practice what is being taught, the learner is unlikely to make the progress needed to pass their driving test. Even after passing the test, the newly qualified driver must continue to practise what has been learned to become both more proficient and confident in their ability. It takes time and effort and some 'going it alone' to get there, but as with learning any new skill, it is worth the effort in the end. There can also be situations that feel harder than others at first, like navigating big roundabouts or driving on motorways. These require additional practice before you can become confident with them. *Remember, nobody learned to drive from reading a book alone!*

Top tip 3: Keep notes

'I was a bit reluctant at first, but I was glad I kept notes as I was able to look back on them, especially when I hit a bump. Developing my own panic cycles was particularly useful as were the diaries and worksheets. I could look back on what had helped me overcome obstacles in the past, so I was able to do some of the same things to help. It also helped me to see just how far I had come in a relatively short time given that I have been living with panic attacks for so long.'

Making notes and understanding your own panic cycle (I will introduce you to this in Section 2) helps learning as you can apply what you are reading to your own situation. This makes it easier to find important points that are of particular relevance to you.

At different points throughout the book, you will see a writing symbol as a prompt for you to make notes. It has already appeared earlier in the chapter when I invited you to identify what symptoms you were experiencing. You might want to use pen and paper or a digital device – whichever you prefer is fine. The worksheets are available in the back of this book or can be downloaded from overcoming.co.uk/715/resources-to-download. When progress occurs over time, it can be difficult to remember your situation at the start. *Notes can allow you to look back and see the progress you are making.* It's sometimes easy to forget!

Top tip 4: Like everyone, expect to have good days and bad days

'It was all going so well, then one morning I got up feeling a bit jittery, I wasn't sure why. I had a bus journey planned but when I was at the bus stop, I started to feel panicky and felt like I couldn't do it so came home. I was

> very upset and felt like I was back to square one. It made me think I shouldn't bother trying. But later that day, I braced myself and went back to the bus stop and got on the bus which helped me get back on track. Although what happened earlier that day threw me a bit, I'm so glad I went back later rather than let it drag on!'

Hopefully, after a short time using this book, you will begin to notice an improvement in your panic attacks. Nevertheless, you are likely to have some ups and downs. Some days will feel easier than others. Don't be discouraged by setbacks – they are normal. In fact, odd as it may sound, setbacks can be useful. We'll come back to setbacks in Section 4. *Try your best to keep at it and not to let how you are feeling stop you from proceeding with what you have been planning to do.*

Top tip 5: Act according to your goals rather than how you feel

> 'It was difficult at times, and I would sometimes think "it's too hard" when I felt particularly panicky. At those times it was useful to remind myself of my goals as it helped me remember why I am doing this and to push on.'

A main focus of the book is to act according to your goals rather than how you think or feel. In fact, this book will ask you to behave in the opposite way to your *'default setting'* which has come about because of the panic disorder. For this reason, a little later in this section you are encouraged to set some goals. You will read more about the patterns of behaviour that maintain panic disorder and how to break these patterns in Section 3. These insights are key to starting to get on top of your panic disorder.

Try not to listen to your thoughts when they are telling you that you can't do this. It is best not to listen to your body symptoms either when you feel panicky – they can be telling you that your symptoms are dangerous when they aren't. Try not to let anxiety stop you from either completing the exercises in this book or doing things that you need or want to do. In so doing, you will find that you can influence your body sensations, and your thoughts, as well as how you feel.

Top tip 6: Let your doctor know you are going to use this book

'I mentioned to my doctor that I was planning to work through the book. She seemed pleased as she wasn't willing to prescribe

> medication and had recommended a CBT approach. She said that I should come back in a few weeks if I was finding it too difficult. I found it helpful to know that not everything was riding on the book and that I could get more help if needed.'

There should be no medical reason to stop you from using the majority if not all the strategies in this book. However, the exercises will ask you to do things that are likely to lead to a certain level of discomfort which can feel unpleasant, and scary sometimes too.

Important: Talk to your doctor to check if they think that any exercises are not recommended for medical reasons (e.g., if you are pregnant, have a diagnosis of chronic obstructive pulmonary disease (COPD) or cardiovascular disease).

It is also important to be aware that medications prescribed for psychological problems (as well as other substances such as caffeine, alcohol and some over-the-counter medications) can have an impact on how you react. For this reason, it is recommended that you make your doctor aware before engaging with the exercises recommended in Section 3 to talk through how this might be best managed. It is not recommended that you stop taking any medication you are prescribed but if you can cut down on your alcohol and caffeine intake (if relevant) that will be for the better.

Top tip 7: Involve family and friends if you can

> 'I recruited my sister to help me, and she was such a great support, especially on getting me started. She also helped with some of the exercises that I may have put off if I didn't have her encouragement.'

Self-help books can be more effective when they are used with someone to support you, rather than alone. This makes sense. We are much more likely to turn up to an exercise class if we have arranged to meet a friend there than if we have not. Equally, we are more likely to hand in work if we have committed to a deadline. There are several reasons for this. First, there is *social pressure*: if you know that someone is going to ask you how you got on with a particular exercise in this book, you are more likely to do it. Second, *other people sometimes have good ideas!* They can help you if something doesn't make sense and can also help you to make the exercises personally meaningful and relevant. This is particularly the case when we come on to some of the exercises in Section 3. Third, *it's good to have people to support you and cheer you on*.

For all these reasons, you are encouraged to find a 'supporter': someone to help you work through this book and share your journey of recovery. Choose someone you trust and see regularly, and with whom you feel you can be completely honest.

Top tip 8: Set time aside to use the book and use reminders

> 'I set aside time every day to work on my panic disorder and agoraphobia. I didn't always manage that but at least five out of seven days each week I did something, which helped me to make improvements pretty quickly.'

It can sometimes feel like a better option to put off exercises because they feel challenging. This is natural and is sometimes called *procrastination*. With this in mind, it can be useful to set some reminders to help you follow through with what you aim to do. This may involve some planning in your day for a few weeks. Calendars (paper or electronic), diaries or smartphones work well for noting when you will do exercises related to your goals. *You could even start now by scheduling time for reading this book!*

Getting professional support

If you don't have someone in your life who can be a supporter, or if you decide that you are uncomfortable bringing someone you know personally on board, you could find a healthcare professional to help you. Your doctor may have information available on who could do this and how you can contact them, so talk to your doctor if you think this might be something you would like to pursue.

However, there is also absolutely no reason why you can't use this book on your own, and many people find books such as this helpful without someone else's input. It may be that you prefer to tackle your problems by yourself. It's up to each of us to find what works best. I hope this book will help you however you decide to use it. Please just keep in mind that professional support should be available if needed and that having a professional providing support can, for some, mean that they are more likely to complete self-help.

Remember, there are no rules about how quickly you should move through this book although it is best to commit to it for a few weeks rather than stop and start. Progress is likely to depend on the time you are able to invest but, for the book to really help, please commit to just two things:

1. Give it a go: read it and try it!

Give the exercises a go and see what works for you. The more you put things into practice, the more likely it is you will reap the rewards. Remember that we all have days when we feel like giving up. Make a commitment to use the book and put the advice into practice, even if you are uncertain that it will work for you before you give it a try. Consider making a deal with yourself to give it your best shot for twelve weeks and see how you feel after that. You can see how far you have got towards achieving your goals at that point.

2. If things get really bad and you think about ending your life, speak to someone straight away

For a few people, when they are experiencing emotional difficulties such as panic disorder and things begin to get on top of them, they can feel so hopeless about matters that they think about ending their life. If things get so bad that you are having these types of thoughts regularly and/or plan to harm yourself in any way, *get help*! There are details of support agencies listed in the back of this book, many of which you can contact 24 hours a day. Let your doctor or other healthcare professional know how you feel right away. *They can help.* Tell someone else, such as a trusted friend or family member. They may be able to support you in getting help. Remember that *you won't always feel this way* and there are things you can do to feel better.

Feeling suicidal at times tends to be closely linked to the experience of hopelessness or depression. It is perhaps not surprising that when people have been living with panic disorder for a long time (especially with the added restrictions that agoraphobia brings), they can feel like they don't want to carry on. Hopelessness and depression can be treated directly or can shift as you make progress towards your goals. When people recover in this way, they no longer feel like ending their life. If you frequently feel depressed, it can be a good idea to seek treatment for your depression first and then, when you are feeling brighter, you will be better placed to start working through this book. If what is written in this paragraph reflects how you are feeling, it is important to discuss this with your doctor. You may also find another book in this series helpful: *How to Beat Depression and Persistent Low Mood*. A list of helplines is also provided at the end of this book for immediate support.

Making change happen

Many people who would otherwise struggle to get going with making the changes necessary to tackle their problems have found the following exercise to be helpful, as it really focuses the mind. Consider the following questions to think about change. You may wish to use Worksheet 4 for this exercise. Please write as much or as little as you like. Afterwards, we'll move on to setting goals you want to work towards.

How important is it for me to change?

Make a note of all the ways your problem has limited your life to date. Additionally, note down how your problem might impact your life in the future if it remains the same or even worsens. How will it interfere with you achieving your life goals? What have you had to sacrifice for this problem? Imagine that you go to sleep tonight, and you wake up tomorrow and everything in your life is how you want it to be with panic attacks no longer a problem for you. Make a note of what your life would look like if this happened. *How would it be different?*

Do I have the opportunity to change?

Imagine that working through this book and all its exercises will take around sixty minutes a day, for up to five days a week (every day if possible), for twelve weeks. To be able to prioritise your work on the problem for these three months, what needs to change in your life? Are there some commitments that you can do less often? Is there some extra support you can enlist temporarily? Can you set calendar reminders? Make a note of what you can put in place to give you the best chance of completing this self-help.

Thinking ahead – setting goals

You've now considered both what your life would look like if it was no longer affected by panic disorder (and maybe also agoraphobia) and the time commitment needed to make those changes. Now let's think about the process of achieving your goals.

The way to do this is to break things down into more manageable and focused objectives you want to achieve over the next few weeks. These goals may be the things you used to do but have stopped doing because of your panic attacks, or they could be new things you would like to do in the future that don't feel possible right now. *Your goals will usually be in keeping with your personal values – things that are important to you.* This will mean that you will be more committed to them and achieving them will have more of an impact on your life.

Setting goals is a great way to identify exactly what you want to achieve by putting into practice the strategies you are going to learn over the following sections. The best goals are:

- Specific
- Measurable
- Achievable
- Realistic
- Time-bound

The acronym for remembering these characteristics is 'SMART'. Setting goals this way can really help when it comes to maintaining a focus on where you want to be, which in turn will enable you to assess your progress. Try to avoid goals like 'I want to feel normal again'. This is a very understandable and reasonable goal. It is also a realistic goal. However, it isn't particularly *SMART* as it is too general and therefore less measurable.

Making your goals SMART will help ensure that you know exactly what you are working towards and when you have achieved them. Being *specific* about what you are setting out to achieve means you will know where to begin to try to achieve it. If you have a goal that is not *measurable*, you won't know if you've met it or not. If your goal is not *achievable* and *realistic*, it may end up feeling like something you've failed at, and that is never a good feeling. If it is not *time-bound*, then you risk losing interest and focus. Let's look in more detail at how to make your goals SMART:

1. **Specific.** Rather than setting a goal 'to be panic-free', think about what in particular you would like to be able to do that you feel you cannot do now because of your panic disorder (and agoraphobia). For instance, you might want to 'Carry on with whatever I am doing when I notice my heart racing until it passes' if that is something you have been avoiding because of panic attacks. That is likely to be a pretty useful goal for someone who is struggling to keep doing what they are doing when having panic symptoms.

2. **Measurable.** Being free of panic attacks is measurable. However, life entails various situations where it is understandable to feel panicky (imagine walking home alone late at night and hearing a rustle in the bushes). 'Being free of panic attacks' also does not say what you will be doing differently without panic attacks on a day-to-day basis. 'Getting the bus regularly' or 'going to a busy supermarket on my own twice a week' are very measurable goals.

3. **Achievable.** Being 100% panic-free for the rest of your life is unlikely to be achievable for the reasons stated earlier although being panic-free on a day-to-day basis should definitely be achievable and what we are aiming for. Instead of *'being panic-free'*, think about what you would like to achieve by the end of this book. To be comfortable being at home alone, going to a high-intensity exercise class, and using public transport alone should all be achievable.

4. **Realistic.** Someone might set a goal of travelling the world without experiencing panic attacks. Realistically, that is unlikely to be something most people will be able to do in three months for practical reasons alone. It's not that travelling the world without having a panic attack is not achievable, but it is probably

not as helpful as a goal that can be just as challenging but can be done routinely every week. Try to keep it reasonably local and something that is currently limiting your lifestyle in some way (panic attacks are likely to have taken over your life on a day-to-day basis), such as being home alone for a prolonged period, being able to go to the shops or using public transport alone or without doing something to make it more manageable (more on 'safety behaviours' later). Mastering situations like these can have the most meaningful impact on your life as well as help you reach the global stuff.

5. **Time-bound.** Try to ensure that your goals are achievable within the timeframe. Do your best to aim for what you want to be able to do in three months' time.

Top tip for goals: It is generally best to write goals positively, so it is clear what you are working towards, rather than what you want to stop doing (e.g. 'spend at least four hours alone at home every day', 'go to an exercise class three times a week', 'go to the local supermarket alone at busy times once a week' rather than 'stop avoiding doing things because of my panic attacks').

When you have decided on the goals you would like to achieve, make a note of them in Worksheet 5 ('My goals for beating my panic disorder'). Now rate each one in  respect of how far you can achieve the goal right now (0 being not at all and 6 being that you can do it without difficulty). The idea is for you to come back and re-rate your goals in one, two, and three months' time to measure your progress. Try to come up with three goals – or more if you like. It can be helpful to make a note in a calendar, diary or smartphone as a reminder to re-rate your goals once a month.

If you have read this section and followed the exercises, you will have considered what your life will be like if you can make changes. You will also have set some relevant goals for going forward. Now let's keep going. Earlier, you were encouraged to make some plans regarding how you are going to schedule in time to begin working on your problem. If you did that, great; if not, try to do that now.

Hopefully, you are feeling motivated and ready to start. In Section 2, we'll look at how to make sense of panic disorder which will lead us nicely on to looking at how to overcome it in Section 3.

Section 2

UNDERSTANDING PANIC DISORDER

People with panic attacks often ask questions like:

In this section, these questions will be answered, and perhaps any others you might have. We'll then move on to look at the ways panic attacks are affecting your life.

Often people seek help for a psychological problem because of:

- **Emotions**, how they feel ('I feel frightened'). Emotions, whether positive or negative, are usually described in one word ('panicky', 'anxious', 'fearful').

- **Body sensations** ('my heart is pounding', 'my chest is tight').

- Patterns in their **thinking** ('Sometimes I think I can't carry on like this', 'It feels like something terrible is going to happen'). Note that just because the word 'feel' appears in the last example it does not make it an emotion, rather it is commonplace to express our thoughts this way. Sometimes people have upsetting images (for instance, seeing oneself collapsed on the floor). When I refer to thoughts throughout the book, this includes images too.

- Changes in lifestyle or **behaviour**, including what they have had to do to cope ('I carry a water bottle with me all the time') or what they can't do any more ('I can't get on the bus to work').

We will look at the role of *emotions*, *body sensations*, *thoughts* (particularly in relation to how they are interpreted) and *behaviours* and how they are connected and affect each other throughout the rest of the book. Making sense of panic disorder is helped by understanding how these connections work.

Before we go any further, let's meet our case examples who we will catch up with again throughout the book. It is likely that some of their experiences will be relatable to you. Over the course of the book, the idea is that their experiences will give you some insight into:

- the connections between symptom areas;
- how the way you view your symptoms can affect your panic attacks;
- the role of 'safety behaviours' in maintaining panic attacks (I'll explain these more fully later in this section);
- some of the challenges faced by people who experience panic attacks;
- and how challenges can be overcome.

Stories of people with panic disorder

It's time to introduce Friya and Darius, who have shared their experiences of having lived with panic disorder, and how they got on using CBT self-help.

While Friya and Darius are fictitious, their stories are rooted in those of real people.

Friya

Friya is a thirty-one-year-old single woman who lives with her son Beau, aged two. Her main difficulty is a fear of having a heart attack, particularly when alone. Her problems started when she was twenty-four, at home alone. She had been out earlier in the day meeting friends for coffee. They hadn't seen each other in a long time so stayed in the café drinking several cups of coffee, which was unusual for Friya. A few hours later she was sitting watching TV when she noticed her heart was racing. She thought this strange, especially as she was sitting relaxing with nothing troubling on her mind. She started focusing on her heartbeat. Soon she noticed other symptoms including shortness of breath, sweating, chest pain, a pain down her left arm, and that she was trembling. She couldn't understand what was happening to her and she became very frightened. Before she knew it, she was having a full-blown panic attack. She lay down and tried to control her breathing and within a few minutes the symptoms passed but the experience left her extremely worried about her health.

Understanding panic disorder 51

Friya visited her doctor later that day for an emergency appointment. Her doctor advised her that it sounded like she'd had a panic attack but to come back if she had any more similar episodes. Friya started monitoring her heart rate for any irregularities by checking her pulse and scanning her body for any discomfort or pain. She was most concerned when she was on her own as there was nobody there to help or call an ambulance if needed. Friya progressed to having occasional panic attacks, mainly when she was alone when they seemed to '*come out of the blue*' for no reason. Each time she would lie down and take deep breaths to control her breathing. After a while, the symptoms would pass but Friya was frightened by them and continued to be concerned there was something wrong with her heart. Eventually her doctor sent her for tests, which came back clear.

After the birth of Beau two years ago, Friya found her panic attacks worsened. She generally felt more anxious and when Beau was six months old, she had a panic attack while driving. She pulled over and put her seat back to do her deep breathing. She managed to get home after the symptoms passed but it left her frightened that panic attacks could happen to her anywhere. On her return to work after maternity leave she had a panic attack when she was alone in the office. She became frightened of the unpredictable nature of her panic attacks, especially when she was alone. She also sometimes woke in the night having a panic attack which was particularly frightening to her due to their coming '*out of the blue*'.

Friya decided to do something about her panic attacks because she was worried that her fear and preoccupation with when she would have her next panic attack was taking over her life. She was also worried that she would not be able to take care of her son.

Friya experienced the following symptoms during her panic attacks:

- Emotions – fear and panic. In addition, she had an almost constant fear of when the next panic attack would happen.

- Body sensations – heart racing, sweating, chest pain, pain down left arm, shortness of breath, trembling.

- Thoughts – 'I'm having a heart attack'; 'nobody will be here to help me'; 'I will die'; 'my son will suffer too if I can't look after him'.

- Behaviour – during a panic attack, Friya would lie down and take deep breaths. Other behaviours included: frequent checking that her breathing and heartbeat were normal, avoiding going for walks alone, and when out with her son she would ensure she was holding extra tightly to his pushchair. She stopped engaging in high-intensity exercise at the gym as she feared it would put extra strain on her heart. Over time her panic attacks were gradually taking over her life.

Friya's goals:

- Goal 1. When I notice my heart racing, carry on with whatever I am doing until it passes.
- Goal 2. Go for a walk alone for a minimum of forty minutes twice a week when Beau is in nursery.
- Goal 3. Sleep through the night undisturbed by panic attacks.
- Goal 4. Go to a high-intensity exercise class for an hour twice a week.

Darius

Darius is forty-two and lives with his partner of ten years, Jasmine. He has been living for fifteen years with panic disorder which developed to include agoraphobia within a few months of his first panic attack. His main difficulty is leaving the house unaccompanied for fear of collapsing. His problems started when he felt light-headed at work. He thought that he was going to collapse after a stressful meeting. He leaned against a wall then sat down until the body sensations passed. The incident frightened him. He went to see his doctor a few days later, who did some basic health checks and could find nothing wrong. The incident preyed on Darius's mind and a few days later he had another panic attack at work. He again leaned against a wall to steady himself before sitting down until the symptoms passed. He feared there was something wrong with him despite his doctor's assurances that he was fine. He visited his local hospital emergency department where tests were run and nothing untoward was found.

Over time, Darius struggled to go to work, finding bus travel extremely difficult, and took a period of sick leave. He was helped to return to work but mainly worked from home. When Covid-19 restrictions came into place the pressure on him to return to the office was removed and home-based working became the norm for his colleagues too. As Covid-19 restrictions lifted, many of the staff remained working from home including Darius. All employees (including Darius) were expected to go into the office at least once a month as a minimum, but the company preferred once a week. Going into the office was extremely problematic for him by then as, although he felt his symptoms came '*out of the blue*' for no apparent reason, he associated them with bus travel and being at work, and he would often make excuses not to go in at all. He was keeping on top of his work at home, but he worried he would lose his job.

As time went on, he was experiencing panic symptoms in other places, like the supermarket, other forms of public transport and the cinema which he had previously enjoyed visiting.

Darius continued to have panic attacks which progressed to happening almost anywhere. He managed them by leaning against a wall or sitting down until the symptoms passed. His life gradually became more restricted as he associated so many places with having panic attacks.

One night during lockdown, while having sex with Jasmine he felt light-headed, feared the symptoms would get worse and so stopped. He did not tell Jasmine what happened and found ways to avoid having sex going forward by saying he was tired or not in the mood. This put a strain on their relationship.

Darius found that his mood was affected by the impact of the panic attacks on his life. He controlled them mainly through the avoidance of situations where he thought he was more likely to have a panic attack or by ensuring he was accompanied by Jasmine, which seemed to help.

With Jasmine's support, Darius finally decided to do something about his panic disorder and agoraphobia because it felt like it had taken over his entire life. He was also concerned about how his mood was being affected.

Darius experienced the following symptoms during his panic attacks:

- Emotions – fear and panic. Like Friya, he had an almost constant fear of when the next panic attack would happen.

- Body sensations – light-headedness, dizziness, trembling, feeling unsteady, sweating and over-breathing (or 'hyperventilating').

- Thoughts – 'I'm going to collapse'; 'I will faint and lose consciousness'; 'I will be ignored, and nobody will help me', the image of himself lying on the floor and nobody coming to help.

- Behaviour – during a panic attack, Darius would lean against a wall to steady himself or sit down if possible, and would often tighten the muscles in his legs while he walked in case they became wobbly. Other behaviours included frequent checking that he wasn't feeling light-headed, including staring at things to check his vision, avoiding going out of the house alone, and always holding hands with Jasmine when out in case he needed to steady himself.

Darius's goals:

- Goal 1. To work a full day in the office at least once a week.

- Goal 2. Travel by bus alone for a minimum of thirty minutes four times a week.

- Goal 3. Have sex with Jasmine at least twice a week.

- Goal 4. Go to the supermarket once a week alone for at least forty minutes.

Friya and Darius's stories show how people can experience panic disorder very differently. Equally, the personal circumstances of Friya and Darius, their ages and lifestyles, are likely to be different to your own. However, the strategies they used to help them overcome their panic disorder (Darius had panic disorder and agoraphobia) are the same as those that should help you. In Section 5, you can read their full stories and how they used CBT self-help to enable them to make changes to their lives. You will find out what went well and about some of the challenges they encountered along the way, and what they did to overcome them. It may not always be easy for you either but reading about others' experiences as well as the challenges they faced and overcame may help you keep on track.

Next, you'll find answers to some of the most common questions people have about panic disorder and I will introduce you to the panic cycle.

Question 1: What happens during a panic attack?

There are two main types of panic attack:

1. Those that are preceded by a period of heightened anxiety (perhaps you are worried about having a panic attack in a place where you have had one previously) or anxiety due to other events or worries (e.g., 'how am I going to pay my bills when my mortgage goes up?').

2. Those that are not preceded by heightened anxiety and seem to come out of the blue. In this kind of panic attack, the person can think there is something very wrong and may go

to a hospital emergency department (this is not uncommon). These panic attacks can be extremely frightening, but they don't actually come *out of the blue*. There will always be a *trigger*, but it can be missed as it is happening inside the person's body. It could be a slight change such as standing up quickly after sitting for a while and feeling light-headed (which is normal). Darius, who believes he is prone to collapse, is more likely to view light-headedness and dizziness on standing up quickly after a while as further confirmation there is something wrong with him. Or it could be that the person has had several cups of a caffeinated drink and feels their heart racing a bit more than normal, as happened to Friya. The changes can be subtle and mild but if the person is experiencing panic attacks, they are likely to be *tuned in* to the most subtle or slight changes in body sensations.

Panic attacks can also be triggered by other emotions to anxiety such as anger as the symptoms are similar (feeling hot, tense, etc.). Some positive emotions such as excitement and sexual arousal (as in Darius's case) also produce similar sensations to panic attacks. These types of panic attack tend to happen during the day.

What about night-time panic attacks that occur when the person is asleep, and which are not linked to bad dreams or nightmares (Friya had this kind of panic attack)? We will come on to these later in this section.

The purpose of bodily changes in anxiety

Anxiety is a normal emotion and an important part of life. It acts as a basic survival mechanism, commonly known as the *fight or flight* response. You may have heard of it. This is our body's primitive, inborn, automatic reaction that helps us prepare to confront danger by either facing it head on (fight) or running away (flight). There are many everyday situations where it is reasonable to experience some degree of anxiety. For example, if you are about to cross a busy road where there is no pedestrian crossing, it is realistic to feel a little anxious about potentially getting hit by a vehicle. In this scenario, anxiety helps to keep us vigilant and to pay more attention to the traffic, thereby keeping us safe. However, for some people, anxiety happens *too frequently* (when they are not faced with real danger), it is *too intense* (it leads to panic attacks) or *lasts too long* (it goes on longer than the stressful situation lasts). So, although anxiety is normal and vital to our survival, in certain circumstances it can be unhelpful and debilitating. This is the case with panic disorder.

> **Important:** Understanding of the fight or flight response and being able to make sense of body sensations as symptoms of anxiety, rather than something more sinister, can be extremely helpful.

Our fight or flight responses are a sign that our body's anxiety system is working but this is problematic if this 'alarm system' is going off when we are not in actual danger. Alarm systems in general can be useful as they protect us from harm by alerting us when danger might be near. Our bodies are pretty good at protecting us from harm in that way too. Unfortunately, in panic disorder, the body's alarm system is going off at times when there is nothing to worry about (a bit like a car alarm when it goes off when someone is walking by rather than attempting to steal it). CBT helps train the body's alarm system to go off only when danger is real.

What happens to our body when we are anxious

Take a look at what happens to our bodies when we are anxious (fight or flight response) and the reasons why. During a panic attack, the body sensations that are experienced are all appropriate for dealing with real danger. In a panic attack you are tricked into reacting like the situation is objectively dangerous, so your body prepares to deal with it. This diagram of the human body shows common body sensations experienced when a person is anxious and the reasons why. This is what is happening when you have a panic attack; your body is reacting as if you are facing a real danger, when in fact you aren't. Did you know that the increase in your heart rate is lower during a panic attack than you would experience if you ran up a flight of stairs? There are enormous health benefits to exercising the muscles in our bodies, including our heart. So, try not to stop exercising if that is something you have previously enjoyed. Another useful fact is that *there is NO relationship between panic attacks and going insane.*

Take some time to examine the body diagram. Which symptoms do you experience? What do you make of the explanations of why the body reacts in that way? Could it be that your body is preparing to fight or flee rather than the symptoms being a sign of something more dangerous?

Understanding panic disorder

Thoughts racing
Harder to concentrate on anything other than the danger and how to escape

Dizzy/light-headed
Excess oxygen from increased breathing to prepare for fight or flight

Dilated pupils
Sight more focused on danger

Breathing quicker
More oxygen to muscles (sometimes over-breathing can result in chest pain but may also be caused by release of stress hormones or increased attention to body sensations)

Dry mouth
Energy for saliva production diverted to muscles

Heart rate faster
More blood and oxygen to muscles

Adrenal glands
Releases adrenaline to trigger these changes in the body

Cold hands
Blood diverted from extremities to muscles

Sweaty palms
Cools down the body

Stomach churning
Blood diverted to muscles causing feelings of nausea or 'butterflies' and may need to 'poo'

Bladder
Contracts from its normal relaxed state resulting in need to 'pee'

Leg muscles tense
Getting ready to fight or run away

Cold feet
Blood diverted from extremities to muscles

Question 2: What triggers my panic attacks?

The nature of panic attacks in panic disorder means they can happen apparently for no reason (out of the blue). *In CBT, however, we don't believe they come out of the blue!* Rather, there are two main triggers to panic attacks – external triggers (from the situation you are in) or internal triggers (sensations happening inside your body). In panic disorder, the person usually develops a heightened awareness of a wider range of bodily sensations.

Internal triggers are the most common kind of trigger to a panic attack in panic disorder and the first sign to the person that there is a problem. People with associated agoraphobia may be most aware of situations that are triggers (e.g., using public transport, standing in a queue, being in a busy supermarket) but will also notice body sensations (e.g., their heart rate increasing as the bus approaches) *so you could say that all panic attacks in panic disorder have an internal trigger as they are the first sign that there is a problem.*

In panic disorders, body sensations are interpreted as dangerous. These are usually sensations that are involved in normal anxiety responses such as palpitations and shortness of breath but which may not have been triggered by anxiety in the first place – for instance, the person might be feeling excited or angry. But as stated in Section 1, our initial thoughts/images (interpretations of body sensations) are not always correct. It is the person's catastrophic thoughts about their body sensations being dangerous (physically or mentally) that leads to a panic attack. In the following table you will see some examples of common catastrophic thoughts about body sensations.

Panic symptoms and the thoughts they are often linked to

Body sensation	Typical interpretation
Palpitations, racing heart, tight chest	I'm having a heart attack. I am going to die.
Breathlessness	I'm going to stop breathing. I'm going to suffocate. I am going to die.
Feeling faint/dizzy	I'm going to collapse. I'm going to faint/pass out.
Racing thoughts, feelings of self or surroundings being unreal	I'm going insane.

Question 3: What keeps my panic attacks going?

From CBT research, we understand how thoughts and body sensations are involved in a panic attack. Let's now have a look at a typical panic attack:

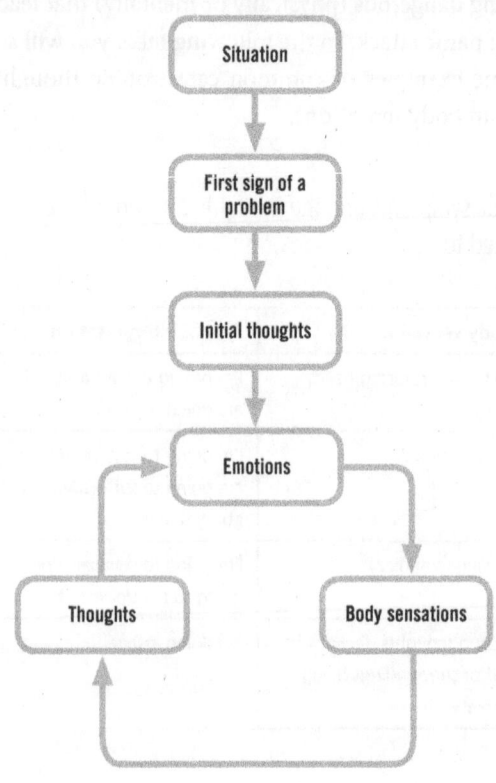

Situation

We start with the situation which may feel like the initial trigger to the panic attack: where you were and what you were doing when the panic symptoms began.

First sign of a problem

An internal trigger (a symptom inside your body) usually causes the first stage of the panic cycle to start. It can sometimes seem that the trigger is external (caused by the situation you are in) but mostly the first sign of a problem will be changes inside your body such as an increase in your heart rate, feeling your breath quickening or becoming light-headed.

Initial thoughts

These are the first thoughts that pop into your mind, which might be something like, 'Oh no, not again'.

Emotions

This way of thinking then leads the person to feel anxious and panicked – anxiety is a natural response to threat.

Body sensations

The anxiety leads to an increase in physical changes in the body (such as sweating and an increase in heart rate) linked to the *fight or flight* response.

Further thoughts

The person then interprets these changes inaccurately, for instance their chest pain, racing heart or light-headedness and racing thoughts as signs that 'I'm having a heart attack', 'I'm going to faint', or 'I'm going insane'.

Vicious cycle

A vicious cycle is then created – a pattern of symptoms that repeats and sustains itself. The distressing thought loops back to lead to more anxiety which then increases the body sensations which heighten the distressing thought (e.g., 'I'm going to die', 'I'm going insane'). Symptoms get worse as the cycle repeats.

This panic cycle can seem complicated. Let's look at what happened to Friya in a recent panic attack to simplify matters. She was sitting watching TV (*situation*) when she noticed a twinge in her chest (*first sign of a problem*). Her immediate response was one of threat – that something was wrong with her heart (*initial thought*). This led to her feeling anxious (*emotion*). The anxiety led to further *body sensations* including chest pain, a racing heart, feeling short of breath and pain down her left arm (all of which are common in people with panic disorder who fear having a heart attack – more on this later). She interpreted these sensations (*thoughts*) as a sign that she was having a heart attack. This made her feel more anxious and her *body sensations* then increased, which seemed to confirm her *thoughts* that she was having a heart attack. The result for Friya was a full-blown panic attack.

Friya's panic cycle

You can see from Friya's panic attack that the situation alone was not the trigger (she often sits on the settee watching TV), rather she noticed a body sensation which she interpreted as a sign there was something wrong with her heart. This led to her feeling anxious and an increase in body sensations that appeared to confirm that she was having a heart attack. She continued round the vicious cycle with her panic symptoms increasing until peaking after five minutes or so. We will look to see what she did next (*safety behaviours*) shortly.

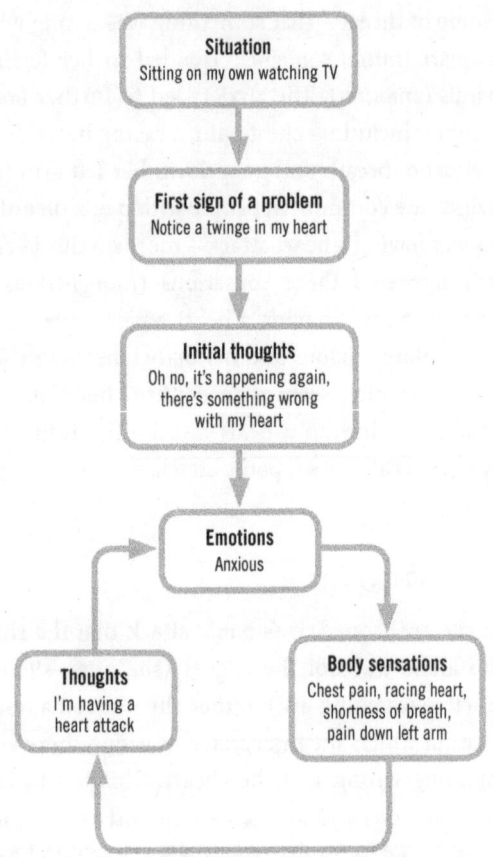

Think of a recent example that is
fairly typical of the panic attacks
you experience. Use Worksheet 6
to answer the following questions
to help you to complete your cycle.
Write your answers in the blank spaces in
the diagram.

- What was the *situation* you were in? Where were you, and what were you doing?

- *Trigger*: What was *the first sign of a problem*? It is likely to have been a body sensation that you noticed.

- *Initial thoughts*: What went through your mind about what was happening?

- *Emotions*: Did you feel anxious or fearful that something bad would happen?

- *Body sensations*: What did you notice in your body (physical symptoms)?

- *Thoughts*: When those sensations were happening, what seemed to you, at that moment, to be the worst thing that could happen?

- *Emotions*: When you thought that, how did it affect your anxiety?

- *Going round again*: What happened as you went round the cycle again? Did the

> symptoms change? Did your interpretation of your body sensations change (thoughts)? What happened to your emotion?
>
> - *Reflection*: Once you have finished your panic cycle can you make sense of how the panic attack started and what escalated it, then what kept it going?
>
> - Once you have your own personalised panic cycle for a recent panic attack, do another one, or more if you like. In some ways, the more the better so you become familiar with what happens in a panic attack.

Once a person has developed a tendency to interpret body sensations in a catastrophic way, two processes contribute to keeping the panic disorder going and making it worse. They are *mistaking body sensations as dangerous* and *'safety behaviours'*. Let's look at these in turn:

Mistaking body sensations as dangerous

In some ways it would be reasonable to assume that thoughts about panic symptoms being a sign of having a heart attack would change if you never died from a panic attack. After all, it would be unusual for someone to survive dozens, if not hundreds, of heart attacks! But it doesn't seem to work that way. Why not? People with panic disorder develop a heightened awareness to the sensations related to their fear and will repeatedly scan their bodies for those sensations. Due to this heightened focus on internal body sensations, the person will notice sensations that happen to us all but which most of us either don't notice or are only mildly aware of and dismiss as being unimportant. For the person with panic disorder who notices these sensations, however, they will interpret them as clear evidence that something is very wrong with them. This can lead them to discount what medical tests tell them.

Safety behaviours

Safety behaviours are a range of behaviours intended to prevent the feared outcome from happening. The person mistakenly believes that what they do to stop the feared catastrophe happening has worked rather than that nothing bad would have happened in any case without doing anything. Lying down and breathing deeply would not stop a heart attack from happening fifty times but because the panic symptoms have naturally passed after lying down, the false understanding that is gained is that it is *because* of the lying down that the symptoms passed.

Escaping from, and avoidance of, certain situations – very common in panic disorder with agoraphobia – are also safety behaviours. The person who gets off the bus early and who then experiences their symptoms pass may well believe that if they had stayed on the bus, they would have fainted or embarrassed themselves in some way. The frustrating thing about avoiding places and escaping from situations when feeling panicky is that (like the other safety behaviours) this removes the opportunity for the person to find out that nothing bad would have happened if they had stayed in the situation. As such, the person gets a bit stuck. Imagine a situation where a child thinks there's a monster living in their wardrobe. If they don't open the door to check, they never discover that it is just their imagination! Avoidance is a powerful safety behaviour that helps maintain the panic cycle as it stops the person finding out that nothing bad will happen to them.

Once a person starts to avoid, a natural process called '*generalisation*' occurs where situations that share similar features with the original situation are avoided as well. So, if a person originally avoids one particular supermarket, they might begin to avoid all supermarkets, shops and department stores. In this way, fear and anxiety grow, affecting more and more aspects of the person's life.

More subtle safety behaviours can occur too even if the person remains in the challenging situation rather than escaping it. These include leaning against the wall and stiffening legs (as Darius did), and gripping a shopping trolley or pushchair (as Friya did). These all serve the same purpose: every one of these safety behaviours stops the person from finding out that the body sensations they are experiencing during their panic attacks are not dangerous at all.

Unfortunately, too, *some safety behaviours can make symptoms worse!* We will come on to some exercises in Section 3 to demonstrate this.

Safety behaviours don't stop there – many people will use them even when not having a panic attack. Friya stopped high-intensity exercising to avoid putting extra strain on her 'weak heart' and we saw that Darius avoided having sex to ensure that he did not collapse during intercourse. Avoidance is a safety behaviour that can also play a key role in helping to maintain unhelpful thoughts about what will happen in a panic attack.

So, as we've seen, safety behaviours are often used in two ways: both to *prevent* you having a panic attack and *during* a panic attack. The following two tables provide a list of common safety behaviours. You can tick those that apply to you.

Common safety behaviours to prevent a panic attack (tick the ones that apply to you)

Preventative safety behaviours	Tick if this applies to you
Avoiding some situations	
Escaping situations if feeling uneasy	
Carrying things with you (e.g., tablets, water bottle, paper bag)	
Making sure you are accompanied	

Common safety behaviours when having a panic attack (tick the ones that apply to you)

Safety behaviours when having a panic attack	Tick if this applies to you
Distracting yourself	
Gripping onto something or leaning on something/someone	
Standing still and tensing your leg muscles	
Moving more slowly	

Trying to control your thoughts	
Taking tablets or having an alcoholic drink	
Controlling your breathing	
Employing relaxation methods	

You may have some safety behaviours that are not listed in the tables. If this is the case, using Worksheet 7, make a list of what you do to prevent you from having panic attacks. Then list the things you do to help make you feel better during panic attacks.

There are endless safety behaviours and although the ones listed in the tables above are some of the more common ones, you may have some that are unique to you. Your two lists will be what we want to tackle going forward to help you overcome your panic attacks.

78 How to Beat Panic

Let's look at Friya's panic cycle again and add in her safety behaviours.

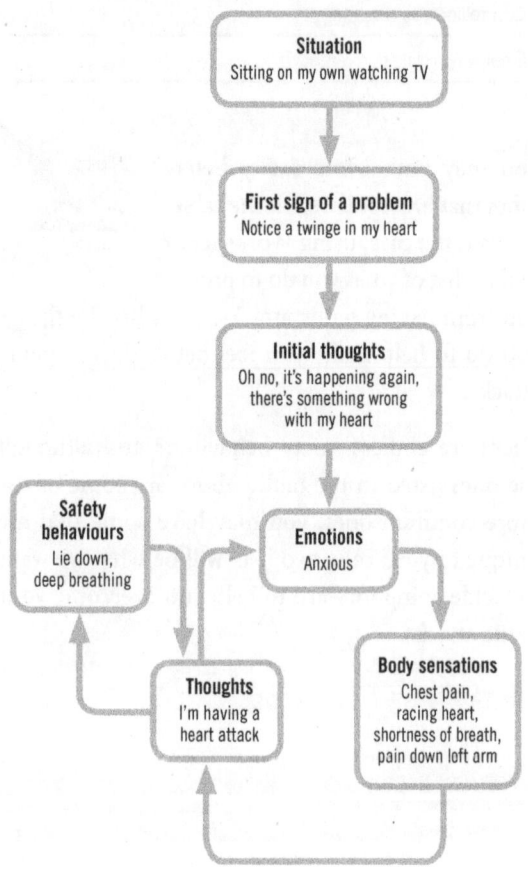

It may seem obvious why there is an arrow from 'I'm having a heart attack' to the safety behaviours (lying down and deep breathing to take the symptoms away) but less clear why there is an arrow circling back to the thought. This latter arrow is there because it is highly likely that the safety behaviours of lying down and deep breathing are keeping Friya's anxious thoughts going. Engaging in safety behaviours means she will never know whether the thing she is most afraid of (having a heart attack) will happen or not. This allows the thought that she is having a heart attack to continue unchecked. *While safety behaviours can help you feel more in control going into a difficult situation, or feel like they help reduce symptoms, unfortunately they are really helping to keep the problem going!*

Add the safety behaviours you engaged in for your panic cycle in Worksheet 6. Now that you have a completed cycle, reflect on whether it makes sense. Also consider whether this panic attack was typical of the ones you tend to experience? If not, please do another one. Pick a particularly bad recent example.

> **Key points**
>
> - Panic attacks do not come out of the blue.
> - There is always a trigger (usually a body sensation).
> - Body sensations lead to a thought that something bad is going to happen.
> - Catastrophic thoughts lead to increased anxiety.
> - The vicious cycle continues, and body sensations, thoughts and anxiety get worse.
> - Safety behaviours keep the cycle going.
> - You don't find out that nothing bad will happen by doing nothing.

If you also have agoraphobia, which is particularly common if panic attacks happen in a public place such as on public transport or in a supermarket, this can result in other unhelpful thoughts such as 'nobody will help me', 'I'll be trapped', 'I won't be able to get home', 'I'll embarrass myself'. These thoughts can be added to your panic cycle if relevant to you. They are additional to the initial thought (e.g., 'I'm going to faint') as they relate to a social consequence of the panic attack.

Question 4: Can I overcome panic disorder?

CBT has been shown to work very well for people with panic disorder, agoraphobia and those who experience both at the same time. CBT is a structured and practical approach that lends itself well to a self-help format. It involves using self-help materials such as this book which provides information about the same strategies you would use if you were receiving help from a healthcare professional. As mentioned earlier, this approach can be used without any support from a professional or friends and family, but having support can be beneficial for many people, especially if maintaining motivation is a struggle. This can be particularly helpful when doing some of the exercises we will be covering later and for keeping up momentum.

Panic disorder is a very treatable problem, and many people make a full recovery, including when it is accompanied by agoraphobia. It's best to do something about it as soon as possible but people who have had panic disorder for years can still overcome it. When panic disorder is not tackled it can escalate and become harder to cope with.

Panic disorder increases the risk of developing other psychological problems such as agoraphobia, due to the avoidance of certain situations or places because of fear they'll trigger a panic attack. This can create a vicious cycle of living in *'fear of fear'*, leading to a person's sense of panic and more frequent panic attacks. Some people with panic disorder develop depression as living with frequent panic attacks can really get you down after a long time untreated. If you think you are depressed, please talk to your doctor and see whether they are happy for you to work through this self-help book in the first instance or if they would like to refer you to another healthcare professional for additional help. You may also find *How to Beat Depression and Persistent Low Mood* (another book in this series) useful to address this problem.

Lots of people live with panic disorder for a long time and may have developed agoraphobia before mustering up the courage to do something about it. Whether you have had the problem for one year or forty years, the tried and tested strategies in this book can help. There is no reason to be less ambitious with your goals either. *Think about what you would like to be able to do and let's go for it!*

Of those people who are treated for anxiety disorders, the majority will stay well. The flipside of course is that there will be some people who will experience anxiety symptoms again in the future (outside of what is normal for us all). There is no agreed way of predicting who will relapse and who will not. What we do know is that people who are able to spot early warning signs that symptoms may be returning tend to do better. This awareness allows people to put the self-help strategies that previously worked for them into practice again to stop these early signs of lapse becoming a full-blown relapse (see Section 4). Remember too that *everyone* will experience fear, anxiety and panic at times in their lives. This is a natural protective response to threat – part of our body's alarm system. So, it is important not to misinterpret normal experiences of anxiety as a problem.

Although it's not possible to guarantee you'll not experience a return of your symptoms of panic disorder and agoraphobia in the future, the tools and techniques in this book will help equip you to get on top of the problem again. These are lifelong skills to help you to take control of the problem. Rather than try to never have a panic attack again, it is much more helpful to keep an eye out for early warning signs that indicate to you (or others who are close to you) that there are signs of it returning.

Question 5: Why do some people wake up with a panic attack?

While asleep, we monitor what is happening around us for untoward sounds (e.g., the parent who wakes as soon as their baby starts crying) and this can include what is going on in our bodies, scanning for danger, which can lead to waking up. This is one of the reasons why we sometimes wake up needing to go for a 'pee' – our body alerts us. A change in breathing or other body sensations is normal during sleep but may be detected during our monitoring when asleep and misinterpreted as being dangerous. This can then lead the person to wake up in a panic attack. If this happens to you, don't worry, the strategies you will learn to use in the daytime will also help with night-time panic attacks.

Getting ready to tackle your panic disorder

Just as it took time for your panic cycle to develop, it can take time to reverse it. This book aims to show you the steps that you can take to make this happen. The biggest step is getting to the stage where you are feeling ready to make the change. You will also hopefully have thought about some goals to aim towards.

Panic diary

As we finish this section, this is a good time to start using a panic diary (see Worksheet 8). The aim is to help you identify triggers to your panic attacks, the sensations you experience, and accompanying thoughts/interpretations, then progress to considering alternative explanations based on what you have learned so far (we are only interested in the first five columns for now; we'll come on to column 6 in Section 3). Going forward, for every panic attack you have, please complete this diary. Here is an example of one of Darius's diaries.

Darius's panic diary

Date	Situation you were in when the panic attack happened and first symptom you noticed	Level of severity of panic attack (0–100 with 100 being the most severe it could be)	Main body sensations	How you interpreted the body sensations (0–100 where 0 = did not believe it to 100 = completely believed the thought)	Alternative explanation and re-rate your negative interpretation of body sensations (0–100 where 0 = did not believe it to 100 = completely believed the alternative explanation)
15.6	Supermarket with Jasmine and notice I am feeling light-headed.	70	Feeling light-headed, dizzy, over-breathing and wobbly.	I'm going to collapse (85%).	
20.6	Sitting planning a bus trip and start feeling faint.	75	Light-headed, dizzy, feeling faint.	I'm going to faint (70%).	

If you have read this section and followed the exercises, you will have examined what happens to you during your panic attacks using the panic cycle. You will also have started filling in the first five columns of the panic diary so you can keep track of your panic attacks as you work through the remainder of the book. If you have done this, great; if not, try to start doing so now.

You are now ready to move to Section 3 where we will look at how you can break the panic cycle and begin to make the changes to your life that are going to make it so much better.

Section 3

STRATEGIES TO OVERCOME PANIC DISORDER (AND AGORAPHOBIA)

If you have completed reading and doing the exercises in Sections 1 and 2, great! Hopefully, you've found the information about panic disorder (and agoraphobia) useful. You are likely to have seen aspects of your own difficulties reflected in what you have read so far. It's good you've stayed with it, and I hope you are reassured that there is a tried and tested way forward to tackle your panic disorder (with or without agoraphobia).

If your symptoms have a different pattern to those described in the last section, it may be you have a different type of problem. If this is the case, and if you have not done so already, please talk to your doctor before continuing further with the book. There are a variety of anxiety problems and panic disorder is just one of them.

If you haven't done so already, this is a good time to come up with some goals (I talked you through this process towards the end of Section 1). These are important as they give you something to aim for and allow you to monitor your progress.

What you will find in this section

In this section we are going to focus on overcoming your panic disorder by breaking into your vicious cycle of panic and trying out a number of exercises that aim to tackle your difficulties and bring about change. This is very much a *doing* section! You will learn about 'discovery experiments' and 'testing experiments' and how they work and be encouraged to try some exercises. In particular, we will look at ways of examining and changing your catastrophic thoughts/images about panic-related body sensations by focusing mainly on your *safety behaviours* and the *thoughts* that lead to them, and how they feed into each other in an unhelpful way.

We will do this by working through a series of exercises and using examples of your panic cycles and the panic diaries you have been keeping so far. There is guidance on what to do each week but don't worry if you find yourself going slightly quicker or slower, just take it at your own pace. You will mainly

Strategies to overcome panic disorder 91

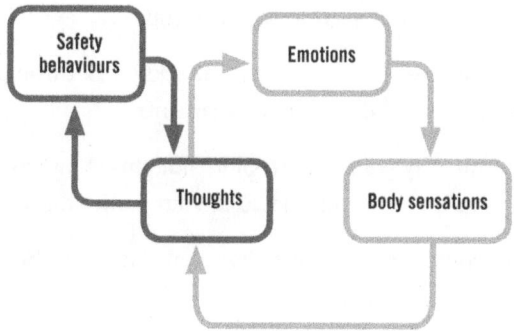

be using the panic diary and worksheets throughout this section. For the testing experiments (see the box below for a useful definition) I will introduce you to a new diary specifically designed for these exercises. Towards the end of the section, I have included some troubleshooting in case you encounter difficulties while working your way through the exercises.

Discovery experiments	Aim to change your thinking about the dangerousness of your panic attacks.
Testing experiments	Aim to change your behaviour to disrupt the vicious cycle of panic.

To sum up, this section will help you:

- discover how your panic attacks work through a series of discovery experiments;
- identify your catastrophic thoughts about your body sensations related to your panic attacks;
- come up with alternative explanations of body sensations;
- and test out the catastrophic and alternative explanations for your body sensations by making predictions and working through a series of testing experiments.

For most of the exercises in this section you will be asked to rate your level of conviction in your catastrophic thought before and after you try out the experiments to see whether there is any change. Please use a 0–100 scale which ranges between 0 being 'I don't believe this thought at all' to 100 'I believe this thought completely'.

You can pick and choose which exercises are most relevant to you and you don't need to do them all or, indeed, do them all at once! I encourage you to try them out and reflect on any learning using the relevant worksheet. It might be that you try an experiment one week and make some changes based on learning from it then try another experiment a few days later (more on how to do this later). You might also choose to do more than one in a day if you are on a roll! Go at your own pace but try to keep up momentum.

Some exercises are relevant for all panic attacks regardless of body sensations experienced and how they are interpreted (thoughts), and these are listed first (discovery experiments 1–5). Please try them all as they are designed to help you start changing your thinking about your panic attacks and their dangerous nature. Others are highlighted as being particularly relevant for certain body sensations and catastrophic thoughts, so please complete them if they are relevant to you. Keep on completing daily panic diaries and the weekly PDSS while you work your way through this section.

Key points

Remember that you are in charge of what you do to tackle your panic disorder. If you are not clear about anything, do go back to re-read the relevant parts of the book again.

Unfortunately, reading the book alone without doing the exercises is unlikely to be enough to overcome your panic disorder

> (remember what I said earlier about learning to drive!).
>
> Research has shown that it can be helpful to have a supporter with you doing some of these exercises. So, if you have someone around who can help, why not try to get them involved? Of course, this should not stop you from trying to tackle them by yourself!

How to plan your time around tackling your panic disorder

There is no right or wrong period of time you should spend on each of the exercises designed to help tackle your panic disorder, but there is a helpful order. Your plan might look something like this, but you may go through the stages faster or slower – do it at your own pace:

Week 1:

1. Develop your understanding of what happens during a panic attack by reading Chapters 1 and 2.

2. Set personal goals.
3. Enlist the help of a supporter if you can.
4. Complete the PDSS.
5. Use the panic cycle to start mapping your panic attacks.
6. Start filling in a panic diary for every panic attack (completing columns 1–5).

Weeks 2–3:

1. Complete the instructions under: **Getting ready to tackle your panic disorder – what you need to get started** (a little further on in this chapter).
2. Try out discovery experiments 1–5 and use the relevant worksheets to record information and any learning.
3. Get your supporter to help you if you can.
4. Continue using the panic diary for every panic attack (completing columns 1–5 and having a go at completing column 6).
5. Complete a PDSS.
6. Choose a day of the week that works for you to review your PDSS and your panic diaries for the previous week.

7. Make a note of the number and severity of panic attacks during the previous week.

8. During your weekly review, make a note of what you have learned about your panic attacks, in particular any change in your thoughts about them – you can record this information in the weekly review form (Worksheet 9).

Weeks 4–5:

1. Continue using the panic diary for every panic attack (completing columns 1–6).

2. Try out any remaining discovery experiments that are relevant to you – this includes the ones specific to your body sensations and catastrophic thoughts. Repeat them as often as you like. It can be helpful to do them more than once.

3. Continue to complete items 5–8 as in weeks 2–3.

Weeks 6–8:

1. Continue using the panic diary for every panic attack (completing columns 1–6).

2. Begin trying out testing experiments that are

relevant to you and build on these as you go (more on this later).

3. Continue to complete items 5–8 as in weeks 2–3.

Weeks 9–11:

1. Review the notes you have made so far in Worksheet 9.

2. Continue using the panic diary for every panic attack (completing columns 1–6).

3. Try out any remaining testing experiments that are relevant to you.

4. Build on your learning by repeating and refining the experiments.

5. Continue to complete items 5–8 that are listed in weeks 2–3.

Week 12:

1. Continue as per weeks 9–11.

2. Read 'relapse management' (see Section 4).

Getting ready to tackle your panic disorder – what you need to get started

Panic cycles

As mentioned, the panic cycle is our starting point. Please ensure you have examples of a recent panic attack, a very severe one, and then possibly at least one other so that you can capture all the information for the three main areas of the cycle:

- body sensations;
- thoughts (your interpretations of the sensations);
- and your safety behaviours related to your thoughts.

Including your first panic attack can be useful too. Try to have at least 3–4 examples, but more is fine too. You can use Worksheet 6 to produce panic cycles that you have logged in your panic diary.

Looking at your panic cycle, can you see any way to break the cycle to help stop your panic attacks?

Why we are not focusing on body sensations

You might be wondering why we are not focusing

on your body sensations. As we saw in Section 2, it is often your *thoughts* about the meaning of your body sensations that make you anxious. This then leads to more body sensations and safety behaviours that you employ to make you feel safe. Research has shown that it is important to *change thinking* in panic disorder and the most powerful way of doing that is by *changing behaviour.*

You may have come up with ideas about potential strategies to control your body sensations such as taking medication, using relaxation methods, distracting yourself (trying to think of something else to take your focus away from body sensations) or controlled breathing (this most commonly involves repeatedly inhaling deeply and exhaling slowly). These could be seen as potential ways of addressing panic attacks but are not without problems. You may be using some of these strategies already. What if you don't want to be taking medication long-term or it is not convenient to do relaxation, distraction or controlled breathing? The main issue here is that panic symptoms are likely to return when you stop trying to control your body sensations, whether that be by medication, relaxation, distraction or controlled breathing.

An alternative (and tried and tested) approach is to examine your interpretations (thoughts) about panic attacks to establish whether they are correct

– you might have come up with this idea yourself from what you have read so far. If this CBT approach is successful (and it is for many people) it will mean you will no longer believe that the body sensations you experience in a panic attack are dangerous and panic attacks will stop without you having to try to control your body sensations by engaging in safety behaviours.

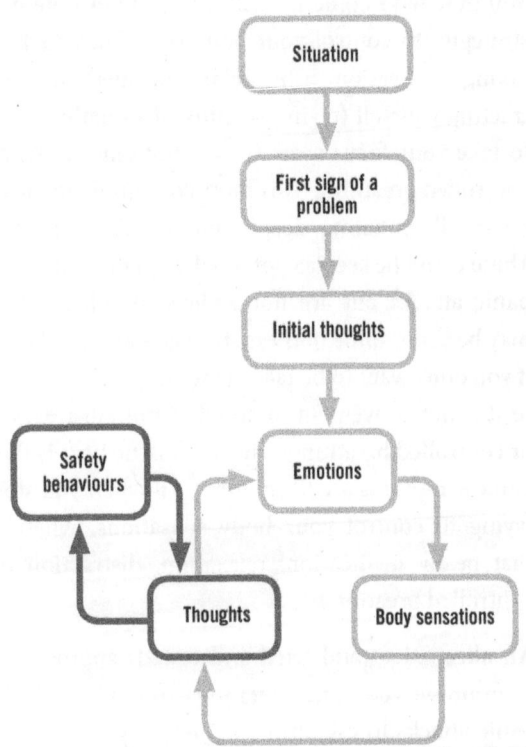

The discovery experiments in this section aim to change your thinking about the meaning of body sensations in panic attacks. These experiments will help build your confidence before we progress to changing your behaviours in the testing experiments. Focusing on these two areas will interrupt the vicious cycle of panic and so impact your emotions and body sensations.

Panic diary

As you work through the exercises in this section that are relevant to you (not all will be), and as you start to consider alternative explanations for your body sensations, begin filling in the sixth column of your panic diary. Keep doing this going forward so you become more skilled in responding to catastrophic thoughts (or images) about your body sensations. We'll come back to the panic diary towards the end of this section.

Weekly reviews

Choose a day of the week that works for you to review your PDSS (see Section 1) and your panic diaries for the previous week. Try to do this on the same day every week if you can by setting aside half an hour or so. Also review any exercises from this section that you have completed in previous weeks and any impact they've had on your panic disorder. It is a good idea to make a note of exercises that were particularly helpful and important learning points from them, including any changes in your thinking about your panic attacks and the dangerousness of your body sensations. It is easy to forget! Where relevant, you can also note down any persistent reservations or doubts you are experiencing in Worksheet 9 that you may want to target over the following week. It is also a good idea to track the number and severity of panic attacks as you go to see whether what you are doing is having an impact.

Discovery experiments: Finding out how your panic attacks work

Over the next few pages, we are going to look at a number of *discovery experiments* that can help shift your thinking about the dangerousness of panic attacks which can ultimately reduce their frequency, duration and how scary they feel. It is worth taking your time to complete the first five discovery experiments. Complete them if you can in weeks 2–3. These are followed by a number of discovery experiments targeting specific symptoms (which you may or may not have). Of these, you should select the discovery experiment most relevant to your symptoms. You can complete these in weeks 4–5 or sooner if you like.

> **Remember:** Rate your level of belief in your catastrophic thought both before and after you try out the exercises to see whether there is any change.

Let's go through the strategies now. The first exercise is important to complete as it will provide an understanding of why you think the way you do about your panic attacks.

Discovery experiment 1: Understanding the role of thoughts and images in panic attacks

Understandably, people with panic disorder tend to try to control their thoughts and images during panic attacks but the reality is that they are extremely difficult to control. For most people, the more we try to think of something else, the more the thoughts or images we don't want to have will intrude. This means that the more we try not to think of something, the more likely we are to think of it! To help demonstrate this phenomenon, try out the following experiment.

For the next couple of minutes (you may want to set a timer) DO NOT think about a pink rabbit with big floppy ears, a white fluffy tail, and a twitchy nose with extra-long whiskers.

It is often useful to get a picture of the rabbit in your mind's eye first before not thinking about it, which is six feet tall by the way. Once you have the image of our rabbit very clear in your mind's eye, do whatever you can to get rid of the pink rabbit. While making sure you are not thinking about our outsized pink rabbit, say out loud whatever is going through your mind, it really doesn't matter what you say. Just, whatever you do, do not think about the pink rabbit! If our rogue rabbit does come to mind, try to push it away and put a dot on Worksheet 10 every time it pops into mind.

Once the two minutes is up, answer the following question:

How often did you think about the rabbit?

Make a note of any learning from this exercise.

Despite these strict instructions to avoid thinking about the pink rabbit, many people find they think about it off and on throughout the experiment despite trying their hardest to push it from their minds. What can we make of this? How does it relate to trying to push thoughts or images out of your mind during a panic attack? Might it be that trying to push distressing thoughts or images out of your mind is having the opposite effect and, if so, could you do something different next time? That might mean just letting those thoughts run freely when they come into your mind. I wonder if our pink rabbit will pop into your mind in future, perhaps later today – let's see!

Discovery experiment 2: What makes me think something bad will happen?

In this exercise we are going to examine why you think something catastrophic will happen in a panic attack. There will be reasons why you think this so let's look at them now.

We are going to think through the things that suggest to you that what you fear will happen in a panic attack will come true. This means looking at what it is specifically that makes you think during a panic attack that you will have a heart attack, faint, collapse, go insane, have a stroke, choke, suffocate or even die.

For many people it is the intensity and seemingly unpredictable nature of the body sensations in their panic attacks that causes them to assume that these things will happen. Sometimes it can be something a person has read, or because of something that happened to someone else ('my uncle died of a heart attack'). Of course, if a person's relative has a heart attack this does not mean they will go on to have one too. If you are one of the many people for whom the main reason you think as you do during a panic attack is due to the intensity/unpredictable nature of body sensations, this is likely to be a particularly important exercise for you.

Using Worksheet 11, think through an example of a recent severe panic attack using one of the panic cycles you have prepared and consider the things that suggested to you that something catastrophic was about to happen. The worksheet includes a column for listing the main body sensations you experienced (column 3) which are likely to have led to what you thought was going to happen (column 4). For instance, Friya found that the intensity of her heartbeat was the most convincing indicator she was about to have a heart attack and when body sensations were severe, they would be accompanied by pain down her left arm. What you thought was going to happen (column 4) should make sense in terms of your evidence for your catastrophic thought (column 5). Keep your completed worksheet to hand as you can use it to inform later exercises.

Writing down the reason for thinking the way you do can be a helpful discovery as you begin to tackle your panic disorder.

Discovery experiment 3: Understanding the nature of anxiety

Understanding the nature of anxiety and why we experience different body sensations is key to overcoming panic disorder. If you have not already read about the role of different body sensations when we are anxious (Section 2), this is a good time to do it. In particular, it is important to know the function of the fight or flight response and how our body sensations serve an important role when facing real danger. They are a sign that our body's natural alarm system is working properly. The problem in the case of a panic disorder is that this alarm system is being activated when there is no actual danger. When people panic, they often interpret common body sensations as being more dangerous than they actually are. The body sensations of anxiety, anger and excitement are often incredibly similar to those experienced in panic attacks. It can be helpful to consider the similarities.

When Darius was younger, he loved fairgrounds – the scarier the ride the better. He would get excited going on a ride, and noted that his heart would race, he would feel light-headed, and his mouth would be dry. At the time, he would not be scared of these body sensations as he was eagerly anticipating the thrill of the ride. However, if he experienced those same body sensations when getting on a bus, they would be extremely frightening. What is key here is that despite the body sensations being incredibly similar, his interpretation of them (his thoughts) was very different across the two circumstances.

The main difference between what is experienced in anger, excitement and panic is *not* so much the body sensations but our interpretation of them. You would be unlikely to interpret the same body sensations as dangerous to you when angry or excited.

Think of a time when you were angry. Use Worksheet 12 to list all the body sensations you experienced. Now think of a time when you experienced great excitement. In the next column,  list all the body sensations you experienced. Now compare these two lists to the body sensations you experience in a panic attack (put these in the third column – you can use the ones you listed in Worksheet 11). What do you notice? What are the similarities and differences? Make a note of these in the table. Many people find that the body sensations are very similar, but their interpretation of them is different. Make a note of anything you have learned from this exercise in the final box. Take a look at Friya's lists and reflections.

This example demonstrates how body sensations can be similar across strong emotions and not unique to panic. The key difference is how the body sensations are *interpreted* during a panic attack. Might being aware of the similarity of body sensations across strong emotions be helpful in future panic attacks? And crucially, if you had these body sensations but didn't have the catastrophic thought (your interpretation), what impact would it have on your anxiety? Your likely answer is that they wouldn't be so scary, so keep this in mind.

Body sensations when I am angry	Body sensations when I am excited	Body sensations when I am having a panic attack
Heart racing	Heart racing	Heart racing
Dry mouth	Dry mouth	Dry mouth
Shaking	Trembling	Trembling
Sweating		Sweating
Shortness of breath		Shortness of breath
Tight chest		Chest pain
Feeling hot		Pain down left arm

What are the similarities across the three sets of body sensations?

Heart racing and dry mouth across all three. Trembling when excited and anxious and more severe (shaking) when angry. Shortness of breath and sweating when angry and anxious. Tight chest in anger a bit milder to the chest pain in panic.

What are the differences across the three sets of body sensations?

Not many, I tend to feel hot when I am angry, and I only get pain down my arm in panic attacks.

What have you learned from this exercise?

There are lots of similarities in body sensations across other strong emotions that I had not thought about before. I don't interpret my body sensations as dangerous when I am angry or excited but do when I am having a panic attack.

Discovery experiment 4: Focus of attention

Many people who experience panic attacks say the main reason they think there is something seriously wrong with them (whether physically or mentally) is because of the various body sensations they experience in a panic attack that they were not aware of before they had panic disorder. You might also have checked with family and friends whether they experience the same sensations. They may say that they are not aware of them, or they might say they notice them but don't think anything of it and the sensations just go away. The difference between you and family and friends is likely to be down to an increased focus of attention on what is happening in your body which your friends and family don't engage in.

Let's consider whether it is anxiety rather than something physically wrong with you that is causing your body sensations, and it is your safety behaviours that are keeping it going (lots of research says it is). That will mean there will be numerous instances where your thoughts about something terrible being about to happen have not come true. Let's look at some examples with Friya and Darius.

Darius was at the supermarket and could feel the symptoms of panic start. He was becoming increasingly concerned that he was going to collapse. He decided to abandon his trolley and leave immediately. As he made his way to the exit, he bumped into a neighbour who had recently lost her mother after a long illness. She had been caring for her mother at home over the last three years. She caught his eye, and he felt he had no option but to speak to her. They had a ten-minute conversation about how she was coping with life after her mother's death. Darius was absorbed by the conversation and his empathy for the neighbour. As he walked away Darius noticed his symptoms had passed. *So, what happened?* Our understanding of the panic cycle tells us that being distracted will not stop a collapse, but it will interrupt the preoccupation and intense focus on body sensations in a panic attack.

Like many people with panic disorder, Friya is aware that her panic symptoms are more likely to happen when she is home alone than when she is out with other people. If we think about this for a moment, let's consider what body mechanism can detect whether a person is alone or in company to trigger a heart attack *only* when they are alone? *There isn't one.* Rather, Friya is more comfortable and less likely to experience panic symptoms when she is with others as she knows she will be able to get help if she needs it.

In both these examples, Darius and Friya's attention to body sensations changes in different situations.

Strategies to overcome panic disorder 113

Darius was distracted by his neighbour and Friya is less likely to pay attention to body sensations when she is with other people.

Can you think of any instances where your catastrophic thoughts during panic attacks have been contradicted? If so, what do you make of that?

Please set aside ten minutes for this exercise. Close your eyes for a couple of minutes and scan your body to notice as many body sensations as you can. Spend this time really focusing on what is going on in your body, head to toe. Once you have done that, open your eyes and pay attention to something near you, perhaps a painting, a bookshelf or a fruit bowl (anything that has some detail) and describe it in great detail out loud. For instance, you might notice different shapes, colour shades, imperfections and blemishes (if looking at fruit), writing and creases as well as different colours (if books on a shelf). Really get into the detail as if you are about to draw it. Do this for up to five minutes if you can. When you stop, ask yourself the following questions using Worksheet 13:

- When you had your eyes closed and you were focusing on what was happening in your body, how strong were the sensations?

- When you had your eyes open and were describing something near you in great detail, what happened to your body sensations?

- If the sensations decreased or you did not notice them after a while when looking at something in detail, what does that tell you about the power of focusing your attention on something external rather than focusing on what is happening to you internally?

People with panic disorder often find that shifting their focus of attention to something external has a dramatic effect on their body sensations (remember the situation where Darius met his neighbour in the supermarket). If there was something seriously wrong with you (e.g. a weak heart), changing your focus of attention could not have that effect. Make a note of learning from this exercise.

Discovery experiment 5: Pairs of words

This exercise helps us consider two explanations for your panic attacks. Explanation 1 is that your symptoms are dangerous. Explanation 2 is that it

Strategies to overcome panic disorder 115

is your thoughts about the meaning of your body sensations making you anxious and leading to more body sensations (e.g., 'my heart is racing so I must be about to have a heart attack', 'I'm feeling unsteady so I am going to collapse', 'my thoughts are racing so I must be going insane').

Let's give it a go. Please read out loud the pairs of words on pages 116–17. This is a list of common sensations and linked catastrophic outcomes. If your sensations and feared catastrophe are not listed, please add them. When you read the pairs of words out loud try to really concentrate on what you are saying and think about their meaning. Dwell on each word before moving on to the next, don't rush it. Ideally, you'll go through the list a few times so do please set aside a few minutes for this exercise.

Once you have finished, use Worksheet 14 to make a note of anything you noticed during the exercise. To help you, please answer the following questions:

- What did you notice in your body when you were reading out the words?

- If you experienced body sensations, how similar were they to what you experience at the start of a panic attack?

- Did you get any mental images when you went through certain words?

- Which words?

- Were some words harder than others to read?

- If you answered yes to the last question, what do you make of that?

Tight chest – Heart attack	Difficulty swallowing – Choke
Dizzy – Faint	Unreality – Insane
Heart racing – Die	Short of breath – Suffocate
Difficulty swallowing – Choke	Numbness – Stroke
Unreality – Insane	Unsteady – Collapse
Short of breath – Suffocate	Tight chest – Heart attack
Numbness – Stroke	Dizzy – Faint
Unsteady – Collapse	Heart racing – Die
Dizzy – Faint	Short of breath – Suffocate
Heart racing – Die	Numbness – Stroke
Difficulty swallowing – Choke	Unsteady – Collapse
Unreality – Insane	Tight chest – Heart attack
Short of breath – Suffocate	Dizzy – Faint
Numbness – Stroke	Heart racing – Die
Unsteady – Collapse	Difficulty swallowing – Choke
Tight chest – Heart attack	Unreality – Insane
Heart racing – Die	Numbness – Stroke
Difficulty swallowing – Choke	Unsteady – Collapse

Strategies to overcome panic disorder

Unreality – Insane	Tight chest – Heart attack
Short of breath – Suffocate	Dizzy – Faint
Numbness – Stroke	Heart racing – Die
Unsteady – Collapse	Difficulty swallowing – Choke
Tight chest – Heart attack	Unreality – Insane
Dizzy – Faint	Short of breath – Suffocate

In the pairs of words exercise you may not have noticed any changes in your body sensations, which is fine and normal. You may have noticed some change in body sensations like the start of a panic attack. Noticing such changes is very common in people with panic disorder (around 80% of people with panic disorder will experience panic symptoms). This tells us something about the nature of panic disorder which is worth thinking about. If looking at words can bring on panic-related body sensations, it shows that just thinking about unpleasant panic-related body sensations is incredibly powerful and how easy it is to enter the panic cycle!

Pause for reflection

Now, if you think of your feared catastrophe, how possible would it be that merely reading or thinking about a word could bring that on?

Discovery experiments for specific body sensations

Now you have completed discovery experiments 1–5, we're going to look at specific discovery experiments for six of the most common fears during panic attacks:

- fainting
- collapsing
- stopping breathing
- having a heart attack
- going insane or losing consciousness
- choking

If any of these fears are relevant to you, please try out the related discovery experiments. Rate your level of conviction in your catastrophic thought before and after you try out the exercises relevant to you so you can see whether there is any change afterwards.

Discovery experiment for specific body sensations – 1. Fainting

Some people feel faint when they have a panic attack. This is very common. The diagram of the body in Section 2 (page 63) shows why you may feel light-headed with a sense of faintness during a panic attack. If you have frequently felt faint or had the thought you would faint but not actually fainted, you may have concluded this is because of something you did each time that stopped it from happening (e.g., sitting down, leaning on something or stiffening your muscles – these are all *safety behaviours*). That is one possible explanation but there is another. The alternative explanation is that the feeling of faintness brought on by your panic attack is due to body sensations in anxiety that would never lead to you actually fainting, even if you dropped your safety behaviours.

> ### Key point
>
> Do you know what happens to your blood pressure when you faint? *It drops.* Do you know what happens to your blood pressure in a panic attack? Your blood pressure *goes up*. This means it is even less likely you will faint than if you were not anxious at all. This was an important point that Darius learned.

'But I have fainted!'

If that is the case, it is important to examine the circumstances when you fainted in the past. Were you anxious when you fainted? If you were not anxious at the time the likely cause is unrelated to your panic disorder. There is only one exception to this rule and that is something called *blood/injury phobia*. A person with blood/injury phobia may faint at the sight of blood or injury. If fainting affects you, the following 'symptoms contrast' exercise may be useful to complete.

In the next table, someone with panic disorder has listed all the symptoms they experience when they faint then compared them to the symptoms they experience during a panic attack. They can then check the presence or absence of all the symptoms across fainting and panic. You can see in this example many of the symptoms are very different.

Symptoms contrast table for fainting versus panic attack

Symptoms when I fainted	Symptoms when I panic
Feeling sleepy	Feeling like on heightened alert
A sense of things slowing down	Thoughts racing
Feeling hot and sweaty	Feeling hot and sweaty
Nausea	Dry mouth
	Heart pounding
	Breathing faster
	Light-headedness

In Worksheet 15 list the body sensations you feel before an actual faint and those you experience in a panic attack. Are they the same? There are likely to be differences. Many people have a sense of slipping into unconsciousness when fainting, while people in the throes of a panic attack are acutely aware of very intense feelings of light-headedness but not a sense of slipping into unconsciousness. If you do actually faint during a panic attack that is unrelated to blood or injury, it is important to talk to your doctor as this is not a typical symptom of panic disorder.

Discovery experiment for specific body sensations – 2. Collapsing

Sometimes people stiffen their legs to steady themselves if they worry about losing balance, falling or collapsing during a panic attack. If this is the case for you, try out this discovery experiment.

Find an area where you can take a good few steps, a hallway perhaps or maybe your garden. Now try to walk in a straight line with your legs tensed so they are very stiff while fixing your attention on where you are walking to. If there is not much room to do this, it might be best to do it a couple of times. Once you have reached where you are walking to, ask yourself: did walking in this way make me feel more steady or unsteady?

Some people find that walking in this way actually makes them feel more unsteady. If that is the case for you, perhaps this *safety behaviour* is making things worse. Use Worksheet 16 to make a note of learning from this exercise including your conviction ratings.

Discovery experiment for specific body sensations – 3. Stopping breathing

Before we try this exercise, let's first look at the experience of over-breathing in panic attacks. Feeling short of breath is a common body sensation in panic attacks. Often people fear they will suffocate or even die. Because of this, when in a panic, many people will try to inhale more air, and some people over-breathe (breathing at an abnormally rapid rate). When we breathe in, we are taking in oxygen, and we are releasing carbon dioxide when we breathe out. Over-breathing can upset the amount of oxygen and carbon dioxide in the bloodstream. This change can lead to dizziness, shortness of breath, a racing heart and can make the person feel like they are going to faint.

Up until relatively recently people who were prone to over-breathing were taught techniques to calm their breathing. This form of treatment is not offered nowadays. For instance, sometimes people use a paper bag to re-inhale the carbon dioxide just emitted. The person holds a small paper bag over their mouth and nose and takes several normal breaths then removes the bag and takes a few breaths, repeating as deemed necessary. Some people have reported this being helpful but there is a lack of research evidence to support its effectiveness.

Although you might find controlled breathing (breathing deeply slowly in and out) can reduce the intensity of your panic attacks, controlled breathing can become a safety behaviour. Panic-related over-breathing is actually harmless and there is no need to use techniques to get it under control – the symptoms will simply pass of their own accord within a few minutes. Safety behaviours such as this help maintain the idea that the symptoms are dangerous, which keeps the fear going. Scary as it sounds, resisting safety behaviours can be helpful to find out that nothing bad will come from doing nothing. The panic attack will simply pass by itself, and your breathing will gradually return to normal. So, if you carry a paper bag for these instances, now is the time to use it for something else!

Let's give it a try. For thirty seconds to a minute, breathe the way you would when you are experiencing a panic attack. Sometimes when people do this, they notice they are having other similar body sensations to those they experience in a panic attack. If this happens to you, what do you make of that? Could it be you are attributing your body sensations to your feared catastrophe rather than it being the harmless effects of over-breathing? After the thirty to sixty seconds, without trying to bring your breathing back to normal, see what happens. In a short period of time your breathing will gradually return to normal without you having to do anything. Make a note of any learning from this exercise in Worksheet 16.

Darius tried this exercise with Jasmine doing it alongside him (it can be helpful to have someone doing it with you), taking conviction ratings before and after. Although he over-breathed for thirty seconds, he noticed no change in his conviction about collapsing and fainting (70%). Discussing it with Jasmine, he admitted that he had engaged in some safety behaviours. Jasmine had not noticed that Darius had been tensing his leg muscles throughout. Darius and Jasmine agreed to do it again. This time he over-breathed for sixty seconds and did not tense his leg muscles. On reflection, Darius was able to see that he didn't need to engage in safety behaviours while over-breathing to stop himself from collapsing. Darius found this exercise useful – his conviction ratings reduced to 30% and his confidence that his body sensations were not dangerous increased.

Discovery experiment for specific body sensations – 4. Having a heart attack

Like Friya, many people with panic disorder who fear having a heart attack describe acute left-sided chest pain and pain down the left arm. It is not unusual to view this as convincing evidence of a very serious heart problem.

Would you be surprised to know that it is only when you experience evenly distributed pain across your chest and both arms that this indicates you have heart problems? Pain that is more concentrated in the centre of the chest suggests angina pectoris (the medical term for chest pain due to coronary heart disease) and pain focused on the left-hand side is more likely to indicate non-cardiac chest pain, which is the most commonly experienced chest pain in panic disorder. *So why is that?*

Many of us have been led to believe that when a person has a heart attack, they experience left-sided pain but as you can see this is not the case. Rather, the link between left-sided chest pain and panic attacks is likely due to a person's understanding of what happens in a heart attack. The person has an increased focus on these particular body sensations while ignoring other information that might be contrary to it. In fact, you are likely to experience pain on both sides of your body at different times, but a person may *selectively* focus on left-side pain as it is in keeping with their understanding about what happens in a heart attack – which is *a myth*!

If the chest pain you experience in a panic attack is left-sided, what do you make of the information about more central pain being most common in heart disease? How might this new information help? Make a note of any learning points from this exercise using Worksheet 17. Friya's conviction about having a weak heart moved from 90% before the exercise to 10% afterwards!

Discovery experiment for specific body sensations – 5. Going insane or losing consciousness

Feelings of unreality are common particularly when people think they are going insane or are going to lose consciousness when having a panic attack. It is a disconcerting feeling, and some people will try to check they and their surroundings are actually real. The person might do this by staring at something, but this can lead to distorted vision. If this affects you, it is a good idea to test whether this is the case with the following two 'unreality' experiments.

First unreality experiment

Put your hand in front of you so you can see it well. You might put it on a desk, arm of a chair, on your lap or even hold it out in front of you. Now stare at the back of your hand without moving your eyes for a couple of minutes. Try to fixate on one point, maybe a mole or a freckle. Stare at it without moving your eyes. While staring at the spot, remain aware of the rest of your hand but don't move your eyes. Notice if there are any changes to the rest of your hand. Does it fade away a bit or seem less solid? Sometimes doing this can make the hand seem almost two-dimensional and unreal. Focusing on one spot can also make the surrounding areas seem unreal. If this happens to you, what do you make of that? This is actually a normal reaction to when your eyes are closely focused on something for a while. If you ask friends and family to do the same exercise you are likely to find they experience the same sensations.

Second unreality experiment

It is not unusual to have feelings of unreality triggered by visual patterns. If this is the case for you, please stare at the picture opposite for a few minutes.

Does staring at this image affect your vision? Do you experience any other sensations? Like me, you might feel a bit dizzy and see the lines moving. What do you make of that? This is normal and there is nothing wrong with you. You might like to

Strategies to overcome panic disorder 129

ask family and friends to do the same exercise to help prove the point. Make a note of any learning from these two experiments in Worksheet 16 and remember to check your conviction ratings before and after.

To conclude, staring at something to help combat feelings of unreality tends to have the *opposite* effect! There are lots of examples of these kinds of illusions on the internet. It is always useful to ask family and friends to check them with you if you can.

Discovery experiment for specific body sensations – 6. Choking

When people have a fear of choking they can notice sensations in their throat and so assume it is closing up. A common safety behaviour is purposefully swallowing to make sure that air can still get down.

What I would like you to do is swallow four times, one after the other. For most people, this is a bit unpleasant after the third swallow and the fourth can seem almost impossible. It can even feel like your throat is closing up.

This experiment shows that the safety behaviour of swallowing can actually result in the outcome that the person fears the most!

Might it be that what you are doing to help feelings of choking have the unintended opposite effect? Use Worksheet 16 to make a note of any learning from this exercise.

Consolidating learning from discovery experiments

Hopefully, you have worked your way through the discovery experiments in this section, both those that are suitable for everyone with panic disorder (1–5) and any discovery experiments for specific

Strategies to overcome panic disorder 131

body sensations that are particularly relevant to you. I hope there have been some important learning points for you in working through these exercises, including changes in the level of your belief in your catastrophic thoughts about your panic attacks.

You will also hopefully have continued to record your panic attacks in the panic diary and taken time to reflect on your panic attacks in weekly reviews. So far, you have been encouraged to look back on panic attacks that have happened in the past week and tried to make sense of them. Many people find this to be very helpful. Hopefully, you have used the worksheets to make notes of your learning points too, as these can be useful to look back on. We will also build on these going forward.

Before we go any further, please look back over your worksheets including any shifts in your conviction ratings and complete the following exercise which aims to consolidate your learning so far.

Using Worksheet 18, make a list of all the evidence you have collected so far that contradicts your worst fears about your panic-related body sensations and safety behaviours. How does your evidence support your symptoms fitting with the panic cycle outlined in Section 2? You might like to go back to examples of your panic attacks that you used in the panic cycle and those from your weekly panic diaries. Please also add the results of all the discovery experiments you tried out. Add what you think is relevant, as there may be other learning to be gained outside the content of this book. Once you have pulled together your list, read it through. What do you make of the evidence you have collected so far? Hopefully, what we have covered has helped start to chip away at any catastrophic thoughts about your panic attacks being dangerous.

Going forward, you can add this evidence to column 6 of your panic diaries, along with any other new evidence you collect. Also make a note of any learning from completing this exercise.

Hopefully, you now feel a bit more confident in your ability to tackle your panic disorder and feel ready to move on to the next step in beating it.

Testing experiments

We are now going to look at ways in which you can collect new information that is relevant to your interpretation of body sensations *during* panic attacks. Hopefully, you will be ready to do this by week 5, or maybe even earlier. Do it at your own pace. We have touched on the role of safety behaviours several times throughout the book, so let's return to them now to explore their effects on panic attacks. As mentioned earlier, and you may have found this yourself with some of the discovery experiments, *safety behaviours can actually make panic attacks worse!*

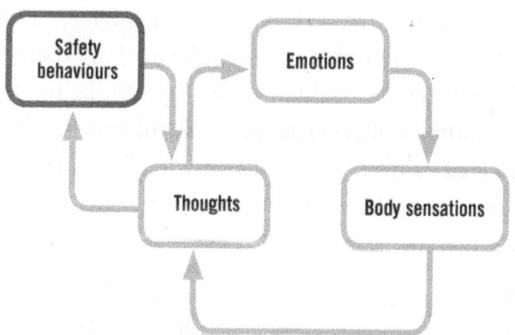

What we are going to look at now are experiments to help show that your *body sensations in panic attacks are not dangerous*. It will involve you experiencing some of your feared body sensations while not doing anything to prevent them from happening (*dropping your safety behaviours*). I appreciate this is likely to sound scary, but these are tried and tested methods that have been proven to help people with panic disorder so please trust me here. We are also building on what you have learned so far in what you have read, and the discovery experiments you have completed. So, let's give it a go. The aim is for you to find out that body sensations may be frightening but they are not dangerous.

If you have someone supporting you while you are working through this book, this is a good time to enlist their help if you have not done so already. Sometimes it can feel more 'doable' when you are with someone you trust at first before later doing it alone. Over the next few pages, we're going to look at a number of experiments, some of which will be relevant to you, and some less so. Read through them and decide which ones relate to you. I will try to guide you in this along the way.

These experiments are a bit different to the ones earlier in this section as you will be asked to make predictions about what will happen. Then we'll look at whether they turn out to be true or false. It is completely understandable if you feel that you want to put the book down and not consider doing such a thing. Please bear with me and remember that this problem is impacting your life in such a way that you must want to do something about it, or you wouldn't be reading this book. You can do this by acting according to your goals and keeping in mind future benefits of overcoming your panic disorder.

Doing testing experiments can feel like a big risk – 'What if what I fear will happen, actually happens?' Sometimes we need to take risks to learn something important. The story of the bricklayer's apprentice exemplifies this well. You may already be familiar with this tale. I am going to use it to illustrate how *safety behaviours* can help maintain thoughts that something dangerous will happen and how testing experiments can help change your conviction in those thoughts.

In some workplaces, it is not unusual for experienced workers to play tricks on new starters. This is the case on our apprentice bricklayer's first day. The apprentice is set to work on building a wall and after a while his supervisor says he is taking a lunch break and asks the apprentice to stay behind to hold up the wall to stop it falling down while the cement dries. The apprentice holds up the wall for over an hour until his supervisor returns. His arms are aching, but he dares not stop in case the wall falls over and he gets in trouble. The question is, how will he know whether or not he does actually need to hold up the wall? While he is pondering over whether he is brave enough to let go of the wall, his supervisor comes back. Of course, the supervisor thinks it's hilarious that the apprentice is still there holding up the wall which would have been just fine if left without support.

What would you have advised the apprentice to do? Would it be to let go of the wall? If you were him, would you have tested it out and let go a little at first to see what happened?

What is the point of telling you this story? Like the apprentice needing to remove his hands from the wall (*dropping his safety behaviour*), this is what is needed for you to find out nothing bad will happen by dropping your safety behaviours during panic attacks. How can the apprentice really be sure that even if the wall is still standing when he lets go, it will definitely still be standing when he leaves it overnight or if it gets windy? Might he be even more convinced it will stay up if he tries to push it over to see what happens? Scary as it might sound at the moment (although hopefully you are feeling more confident now you have got to this stage of the book), not only do you need to let go of your wall (drop your safety behaviours), I want to help you give that wall a good hard push so you can feel totally convinced that nothing bad will happen in your panic attacks!

Testing experiment diary

I mentioned at the start of this section we would use a different diary for the testing experiments. Collecting evidence to contradict your thoughts that something dangerous is going to happen in your panic attacks is a crucial step in beating your panic disorder. Testing experiment diaries help as they provide a useful reminder of progress and key learning points. The idea is to always complete the first three sections of the diary in Worksheet 19 before any testing experiment, and the remaining five sections afterwards. We will now look at some examples of testing experiments. Yours will be unique to you, but the following examples may help you come up with some ideas. We will start by looking at how Friya used the diary.

Testing experiment – Fear of having a heart attack

Like many people with panic disorder, Friya avoided high-intensity exercise in case the increase in her heart rate would lead to a panic attack, or worse, she would have a heart attack. Friya's conviction that her panic attacks would lead to a heart attack had already reduced following her completion of and reflections on the earlier discovery experiments. Understandably, however, she still had some worries about completing the testing experiments.

The first step in this testing experiment is to make a prediction. Friya predicted that if she engaged in strenuous exercise for more than a minute, she would have a heart attack. She thought of a number of ways she could test this prediction and listed them in the testing experiment diary in order of difficulty. The first testing experiment involved her and her friend Jen running up and down the stairs in her house for five minutes, five times the amount of time she thought would be required to prove that she would not have a heart attack (testing letting go of the wall!). Both their hearts were soon racing, and they felt breathless. She set a timer and when it went off at five minutes she stopped, as did her friend. Importantly, as well as not engaging in any safety behaviours before the experiment (slowing down to control her heart rate or controlling her breathing), Friya committed to not engaging in any safety behaviours immediately afterwards as well, such as lying down and deep breathing.

After the five minutes, neither Friya nor Jen had a heart attack. Rather, Friya and her friend had the exact same sensations of being out of breath, and their hearts were racing. It took a couple of minutes for their breathing to return to normal naturally, but more quickly than would be the case if Friya had engaged in deep breathing. Friya completed the rest of the sections in the testing experiment diary. Importantly, this experiment resulted in Friya realising that she did not need to do anything for her breathing to return to normal and she felt significantly more confident that she would not have a heart attack by engaging in high-intensity exercise. Friya and Jen did a similar experiment the next day when they went for a twenty-minute run. You can see how doing this experiment with a friend helped Friya. She could compare sensations with Jen, which 'normalised' the experience and shook her firmly held conviction that prolonged exertion would lead to a heart attack.

Friya's testing experiment diary

Testing experiment diary
Date: 4th March
Preparation for experiment
My catastrophic panic thought: If I put strain on my heart I will have a heart attack
Strength of conviction (0–100%): 80%
Ideas for experiment to test the catastrophic panic thought (circle the best one). Remember it is vital you do not engage in any safety behaviours so include this in your ideas. 1. ⟨Run up and down the stairs⟩ 2. Go for a twenty-minute run with friend 3. Go for a twenty-minute run on my own 4. Go to a high-intensity gym class
Specific predictions about what will happen in this experiment, how you will know if your prediction is true, and your strength of conviction (0–100%). **Prediction:** If I exert myself for longer than a minute I will have a heart attack. **How I will know if my prediction is true:** I will collapse on the stairs and Jen will have to call an ambulance. **Strength of conviction (0–100%):** 75%

Strategies to overcome panic disorder 141

Post-experiment analysis
Describe the experiment you carried out and whether you engaged in any safety behaviours:
I ran up and down the stairs with Jen behind me doing the same. I was tempted to stop at times, but Jen cheered me on and that pushed me to continue. Jen noticed I was holding my chest at times (a safety behaviour) and pointed it out, so I stopped doing that. I got out of breath quite quickly, and worried that might not be normal but Jen was the same. By the end of five minutes, it wasn't so much of a run but a walk as we were both so out of breath.
Did your prediction come true?
No!
Re-rate your conviction in your original thought: 20%
What have you learned from the experiment and how likely do you think it is that your original prediction will happen sometime in the future?
My heart can cope with exertion. My heart is as likely to be able to cope with strain as anyone else's. It is my preoccupation with sensations in my heart and doing deep breathing that is keeping my panic attacks going.
What else can you do to test your original prediction?
Go for a run with Jen and if that goes well, go for a run on my own.

How might doing a testing experiment like this help you address some of your fears about exercise? If you avoid exercising, this is a relevant experiment for you. First make a prediction and work out how to test it. Then give it a go, preferably with some support in the first instance. Be sure to use the testing experiment diary in Worksheet 19 as this is important for recording what you predict will happen, what you do, and being able to reflect on the experience afterwards to learn from it.

Testing experiment – Fear of going insane

If you are someone who worries about going insane during a panic attack you may find this next testing experiment helpful.

If this type of fear affects you, you may feel that you must keep tight control of racing thoughts to prevent you from going insane. With a supporter if possible, try to bring on the thoughts and sensations you see as a sign you are going insane. For instance, a person might have images of themselves in a straitjacket or locked up in a tiny room with no window. Rather than try to control your thoughts and sensations like you might usually do, ensure that you just let them go and don't do anything to control them. In fact, if you can, try to make them worse by purposefully bringing to mind the thoughts you try to push away! You might be anxious about trying this so you can ask your supporter to go first then follow them. Using the testing experiment diary (Worksheet 19), make a prediction of what will happen before the experiment. Afterwards, on reflection, what did you find out? The reality is that it is impossible to make yourself go insane. Next time, try it on your own and do it for longer to *push the wall*!

Testing experiment – Fear of stopping breathing

If you are someone who gets short of breath in a panic attack and are concerned that you will stop breathing, this experiment is for you.

Sometimes people will make a concerted effort to breathe and are extremely conscious of breathing in and out. What do you think would happen if you did not purposefully breathe? What happens when you are asleep? Make a note of your prediction in the testing experiment diary (Worksheet 19).

Breathing is *reflexive* so if you try to stop breathing it is not possible. Give it a try. Do it with a supporter if you can. Now take a breath and hold it for as long as you can. Try your hardest to stop breathing. You might be able to do this for a minute or more, but your lungs will force you to breathe out and then in again. What did you learn from doing this exercise? Make a note in the testing experiment diary. How might it change what you do in a panic attack going forward? Might following this up with doing the experiment alone help you *push the wall*?

Testing experiments for avoidance

As is common in panic disorder you may also have accompanying agoraphobia like Darius. Once you have worked through all the discovery and testing experiments presented so far that are relevant to you, these additional testing experiments are important to do if you have found yourself avoiding things or situations because of your panic disorder. These experiments are designed to enable you to live your life more freely. When you have panic disorder with agoraphobia you will find you avoid or escape situations to reduce the chance of having a panic attack. Living in this way can be very restricting. When you do go into feared situations you may engage in numerous safety behaviours to stop panic attacks from happening (e.g., hanging onto something, taking something or someone with you to feel safer). Here, our focus is firmly on safety behaviours.

There may be some situations you find it almost impossible to imagine entering. If this is the case for you, leave those situations aside for now and concentrate on situations you are willing to try, even though they still cause you some anxiety. It is better to have early successes with relatively easier situations to help build your confidence before entering the situations that may seem impossible right now. Even though it will be difficult, you are in complete control of planning the testing experiments to test out your thoughts that something bad will happen.

First, make a list of situations and places you tend to avoid and if possible, categorise them from moderately difficult to what feels impossible at present using Worksheet 20. We will focus on the moderately difficult ones first. Once you have built up your confidence, you can tackle the ones that currently feel impossible. At that point, they will seem more manageable.

Here's Darius's list of avoidances:

My avoidances
Moderately difficult
Going to the supermarket with Jasmine and separating for a few minutes at a time
Having sex with Jasmine
Going for a walk in the local area alone
Extremely difficult
Bus travel alone
Going to the supermarket alone
Working in the office

Testing experiments involve both going into situations where panic sensations tend to occur and not using safety behaviours to help you cope when panic symptoms start. These situations may be avoided altogether or only done in the company of others and/or include safety behaviours to make them feel 'doable' (e.g., holding onto something or carrying something with you). The aim of doing testing experiments is for you to discover that what you fear will happen (e.g., having a heart attack or fainting) will not happen in reality. I'm sure this sounds incredibly scary, but you can do it. It's all part of not only letting go but also building up to *pushing the wall*!

Darius worried that if he went to the local supermarket alone, he would collapse and lose consciousness. First, he made a prediction – if I go into a supermarket and don't stiffen my legs and use a shopping trolley to steady myself, I will collapse. Despite all of the learning he had gained from the discovery experiments he was still too frightened to go alone so he went with Jasmine. They agreed she would wander off to different aisles and leave him by himself for a few minutes at a time. When Darius began to feel anxious, he would move away from the trolley and ensure he did not stiffen his legs. By doing this, he discovered his prediction had been mistaken; he did not collapse. The next time they

Strategies to overcome panic disorder 147

went to the supermarket, Jasmine stayed outside in the car. The time after that, Darius went alone as he had built up his confidence.

As mentioned previously, it is not uncommon for people with accompanying agoraphobia to have additional worries about embarrassing themselves if they have a panic attack in public. Often these concerns are about the person making a fool of themselves in some way. These kinds of concerns lend themselves well to testing experiments. Darius predicted that if he collapsed in a supermarket people would step over him or think he was weird and give him a wide berth.

Have you ever been in a public place, and someone has fainted or collapsed? What happened? Most people, if they have observed this, say that people nearby come to help, and the affected person is given something to sit on and a glass of water. Then when the person feels back to normal, they can go on their way or medical help is called. If you have a supporter, they may be willing to pretend to faint or collapse in a public place so you can observe what happens. Jasmine agreed to do just that and pretended to collapse in a supermarket while Darius watched from a distance. A member of staff came to her and offered a chair and a glass of water. Other shoppers glanced to see what was going on and two went over to chat to her. After a few minutes, everyone had gone about their business. Jasmine then got up and walked away. By recording and reflecting on the results of this experiment, Darius was able to take away new learning that helped reduce his fear of the social consequences of a collapse.

Darius also worried that if he was a long way from home, he wouldn't be able to find his way back. Once Darius had increased his confidence closer to home with testing experiments, he went on a journey to a town he had not been to before. He had in mind that if he got lost, he could ask someone for directions and made a point of noticing key landmarks, such as a pub beside the bus stop. While he was there, he did experience panic-related body sensations but not a full panic attack. He also got a bit lost when he decided it was time to go home but he asked for directions from a stranger who was able to help him find the bus stop. Darius kept a diary of the testing experiment and was able to take lessons from the experience that made him feel more confident about leaving home alone.

Addressing avoidance of situations using testing experiments is vital to show that those situations are not dangerous. However, I would always recommend doing the earlier discovery experiments first. This is because doing the earlier exercises will mean

Strategies to overcome panic disorder 149

you will already have made some useful discoveries about your panic-related body sensations and the unhelpful impact of your safety behaviours before entering feared situations.

Remember, the aim of testing experiments is to test out your predictions of what will happen (e.g., 'I will faint'). In an experiment like this there are certain things to do before, during and afterwards. Use your testing experiment diary to help with this (Worksheet 19).

Before:

- Consider the evidence for and against your prediction by reviewing what you have learned so far from previous experiments in this section (refer to what you wrote in Worksheet 18).

- Complete the first three sections of the testing experiment diary.

- Include in the diary the safety behaviours you would usually engage in (e.g., holding onto things, trying to control your mind) and commit to not doing them.

- Consider using coping statements on flash cards to help you remember the evidence against your prediction before entering the situation – some people find these very useful (more about these later).

During:

- Do not measure your anxiety levels – it is almost certain you will feel anxious so there is no need to make a note of that. Rather, focus on what you fear will happen and whether it happens. After all, if you do not think anything bad will happen, you will not get anxious. *Thoughts rather than level of anxiety are key here!*

After:

- Complete the final sections of the testing experiment diary. If your prediction did not come true, why not? If you believe your prediction did not come true because you didn't have much in the way of body sensations or you were engaging in safety behaviours, plan to do it again, the sooner the better. Next time try to increase the level of challenge in the experiment (e.g., if it was very quiet in the supermarket, go at a busier time; if you held onto a shopping trolley, use a basket next time).

> ### Top tip
>
> When doing testing experiments, in addition to dropping safety behaviours, it can also be a good idea to purposefully exaggerate your symptoms. For example, when Friya returned to high-intensity exercise classes she purposefully exercised more intensely to increase her breathing and heart rate in an attempt to make her chest feel tighter. Darius leaned over to pick up an item while standing on one leg. Going that bit further provided them both with additional proof that their catastrophic thoughts would not become reality. Just like the apprentice, they were trying to *push the wall over*.

Additional practice opportunities

You may experience panic symptoms outside of the testing experiments. If this happens, try your best to resist engaging in safety behaviours. Instead, use these episodes as an opportunity to do some testing and note any learning from the experiences.

> ### Pause for reflection
>
> If you have been busy engaging in testing experiments, review your diary weekly. You can do this alone or with your supporter if you have one. When reviewing how the testing experiments have gone so far, plan to build on this to test your unhelpful thoughts further. As you gain confidence, move from moderately difficult situations to the extremely difficult ones. Do this throughout weeks 9–12 and don't forget that you are not only letting go of the wall, but you also want to give it a good shove!

> ### Key point
>
> It can take a few weeks of testing experiments to fully gain confidence that nothing bad will happen by doing things you have been avoiding because of your fears.

Troubleshooting

It is unlikely that overcoming your panic disorder in this way will all be plain sailing! If it is, then great! But you might get a fright and want to stop tackling your panic disorder. That is normal. Try to look on setbacks as learning opportunities. You might even go back a step in the programme to build up your confidence again. The key thing is to not stop but keep on going so you can *let go of the wall* until you feel confident enough to try to *push it over*. Let's take a look at some of the setbacks you might experience.

I am frightened I won't be able to cope with my anxiety when trying out the experiments

This concern is not uncommon. It can feel like a big thing to do the opposite of what you currently do in panic attacks. Some people find it helpful to use coping statements on flash cards. These are phrases you can say to yourself or write down on a piece of card. Often writing them down for the first few weeks of the treatment is helpful. Then try *saying* them to yourself. For example, they may include things like 'Panic attacks are extremely unpleasant, but they won't harm me' or 'These feelings will pass'. Come up with your own that you think will help. It is vital that your coping statement is relevant to *you*. Here's what Darius used as one of his coping statements:

> *Remember why you are doing this. You CAN do it!*

I had a panic attack when trying a testing experiment and I am too frightened to give it another go

Panic attacks, while not at all dangerous, are horrible to experience. Try to remember that body sensations are escalating because you are interpreting body sensations in a catastrophic way. Remind yourself they will pass without you having to do anything at all. If this happens to you, review the learning from the early discovery exercises. By taking a step back, you can begin to work up to more ambitious experiments again.

I have been progressing well through the discovery experiments on my own but now I feel like I need someone to support me with the testing experiments, and I don't have anyone I can ask

If this happens to you, please contact your doctor who will be able to help you access a healthcare professional. Having a supporter helps and a healthcare professional can act in this role for you and also offer you any guidance that you might need.

I want to overcome my panic disorder, but other things are getting in the way

Perhaps the time is not right for you to start tackling your panic disorder. You might like to return to the 'Making change happen' section of Section 1 and consider the questions 'How important is it for me to change?' and 'Do I have the opportunity to change?' If now isn't the best time, don't worry. Come back to it when you have more space in your life to give it a go. Keep the book so you can use it at a time that is right for you.

Summing up

There has been a lot to think about and try out in this section and I wonder how you feel about it. It is a lot to take in! You may want to read this section more than once. You might be feeling a bit overwhelmed at the idea of facing some challenging situations and dropping safety behaviours. Perhaps some experiments jumped out more than others as being relevant to you. Please try the relevant discovery experiments earlier in the section to help build up your confidence before trying out the testing experiments.

It is important to use your learning from trying the experiments in this section to inform your alternative explanations for panic-related body sensations in your panic diaries (Worksheet 8). The idea is to use this learning to help you feel more confident to drop safety behaviours going forward when you experience feared body sensations. If you experience any unexpected panic attacks or increases in body sensations, always try to resist engaging in safety behaviours and complete all six columns of the panic diary so you can review what happened and learn from the experience.

Continue to use your panic diaries for any panic attacks you experience and ensure you complete the last column, so you are continually chipping away at your catastrophic interpretations. Have you noticed any difference in the frequency or severity of your panic attacks? It is a good idea to track this in your weekly reviews alongside any changes in your PDSS. Over the later weeks you should notice a reduction in the frequency and severity of your panic attacks.

By the time you consider the more challenging testing experiments, they will seem a bit less difficult as you will already have chipped away at your interpretations of body sensations in panic attacks. And remember, like the bricklayer's apprentice, you need to be a bit brave to find out that *what you fear will happen won't actually happen*.

Please carry on using the strategies in this section until you conquer your panic attacks. Although it is likely you will need to engage in the exercises in this section for up to twelve weeks, if you are still experiencing the same level of difficulties after six weeks of using the CBT strategies in this book please talk to your doctor. It may be you would benefit from a healthcare professional helping you tackle your panic difficulties.

If you are now feeling free of your panic attacks and want to see how to stay well, move on to how to maintain these gains in Section 4.

Section 4

THE RELAPSE MANAGEMENT TOOLKIT

Hopefully, by now you have a better understanding of some of the factors that have been keeping your panic disorder going and have made changes to how you have previously been dealing with these difficult body sensations and situations. Most of all, I hope you are feeling better and that you are able to do more and live life without panic attacks hampering your enjoyment of things you want to do.

If you have worked your way through this book and panic attacks are still interfering with your life, please seek help from your doctor. This problem is still surmountable. It may just be that you need professional help to get you there.

If you have made improvements, that's fantastic. Hopefully, you are now making progress towards meeting the goals you made earlier in the book (we'll revisit these later). Please continue to use the strategies you have learned. You should find your panic attacks will decrease and hopefully disappear.

CBT self-help books like this have helped lots of people overcome their problems. The majority of those people stay well. However, as mentioned in Section 2 it is also natural that you may experience the occasional setback on your road to recovery: a time when you might find it harder to do the things you want to do without feeling panicky.

Through your own hard work, you have successfully helped yourself to feel better. Now we need to keep an eye on this and check you don't slip back into the panic cycle again. This is the final stage – staying well and dealing with any difficulties you may encounter in the future. To increase the chances of you staying well, please work through this section. You've worked hard and now it's important to maintain what you have gained.

You may want to just give this book to a charity shop as you are done and dusted with it but please don't, not yet, if ever! Or you may worry you will lose some of the progress you've made or worry about your panic attacks coming back again in the future (this is called a 'relapse'). You might have some questions such as:

The relapse management toolkit

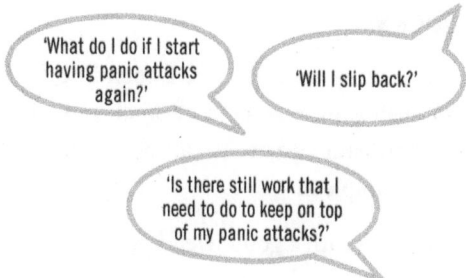

'What do I do if I start having panic attacks again?'

'Will I slip back?'

'Is there still work that I need to do to keep on top of my panic attacks?'

Once you begin to feel better, understandably you want to maintain the positive changes you've achieved. It can be frightening to think you might slip back, and your life becoming limited by panic attacks again.

If a healthcare professional has supported your efforts using this book, being discharged from their care may produce concerns for you about whether you can now cope alone. Please remember that it wasn't the support from the professional that resulted in your progress. Rather, it was the result of the hard work *you* put into using the strategies from this book supported by the practitioner. It was *your* application of the knowledge and techniques *you* have learned in this book that produced your recovery. You can successfully apply these techniques in the future if you need to. The use of this toolkit will help you to keep on track.

Setbacks

Life is full of ups and downs. Depending on how you are feeling, even something small can trigger a setback. Stressful situations can often cause problems, for example if:

- you argue with a good friend;
- you or a loved one becomes ill;
- your children are sitting exams;
- you apply for a job and don't get it;
- your finances are stretched;
- or you experience a bereavement.

The possibilities are endless. You may even experience a one-off panic attack triggered by these stressful situations. Many people would. That does not mean you are back to square one, far from it.

What is important is identifying the situations that might lead to a setback and planning how you can deal with these situations before they cause problems. Some setbacks can't be anticipated and planned for. So, it is important to know the warning signs so you can identify when a setback might be about to begin. Then you can put in place a plan for how to cope. This will mean that the setback is short-lived and as mild as possible. In Section 5 you will read about Friya and Darius's setbacks and how they dealt with them.

Have you noticed any fluctuations in your symptoms of panic or periods when the frequency was greater since they started? Casting her mind back Friya noted that she had a worsening of symptoms following a news item about a footballer who died on the football field from a heart attack. Darius linked being in work with collapse and noticed a significant improvement in his symptoms when he began working from home, although later his symptoms happened in other places too.

At stressful times, you may begin to experience some unpleasant body sensations and thoughts about something catastrophic happening. This might lead to you engaging in safety behaviours such as avoiding situations again that were related to your panic attacks. This is termed a 'lapse' – a temporary return of symptoms. You may then worry that you are going to 'relapse', and your problem will return.

What's the difference between a lapse and a relapse?

A *lapse* is a brief return to feeling more fearful or engaging in safety behaviours such as avoiding situations again in a way that might interfere with your life. Lapses are normal and occur occasionally. So long as you put into practice the strategies you have learned, you can quickly get back on track.

A lapse can become a *relapse* if it is allowed to take hold. This is where problems return on a longer basis. The panic cycle starts up again. If you also have agoraphobia, you will find you are avoiding going to certain places again. This will begin to significantly interfere with your lifestyle once more. The difference this time is you now have the knowledge and skills to reapply the strategies you have learned to help you recover. You know the principles of CBT and how it works.

You may begin to feel hopeless about things which will worsen matters. Try to be patient and compassionate with yourself. See a lapse for what it is: just a temporary 'blip'. Try not to let it undermine your confidence by thinking of the worst-case scenario. If you do think negatively in this way, it may mean you switch into the panic cycle again. Try not to engage in safety behaviours including avoiding situations. The task of recovery is easier if you catch it quickly before old habits become engrained into your lifestyle again. This is the reason why it is helpful to learn to notice the early warning signs (or 'red flags') that indicate things may be slipping backwards.

If possible, try to keep doing all the things you have managed to achieve. If some situations have become a bit more difficult, get going with entering them again to build up your confidence. This will help prevent a lapse from becoming a relapse. Don't give up. You know what works for you. Reapply the strategies and they will help you again.

> **Important:** Setbacks and lapses may occur. Be realistic: you are likely to experience them at times. Recognise them for what they are and not as a sign you have gone back to square one.

You have the tools to prevent a lapse from becoming a relapse. You know the function of the body sensations. You know how to overcome your panic attacks if they persist. Please don't imagine a 'doomsday' scenario where all your problems are flooding back. Try to:

- keep things in proportion and remember you have the tools to overcome any issues if need be;

- keep a check on increased focus of attention to body sensations and don't engage in safety behaviours as they keep the problem going;

- and maintain a pattern of behaviour where you are generally approaching situations relating to your panic attacks rather than starting to avoid them again.

If you have a lapse, try going back through Section 3 and reapplying the strategies. This is likely to increase your confidence and help you get on top of your panic attacks before things build up.

Hopefully, you will have learned from using this book that CBT strategies are available to help you to help yourself. These can continue to be put into action in the future if you feel the need to do so. Making a relapse management plan and putting it into action when needed reduces the likelihood you will slip back and your panic attacks return. It will also ensure you have the confidence to spot any early warning signs or 'red flags'. This insight will allow you to get on top of any symptoms as they occur.

You can think of this section as a toolkit to help you:

- recognise red flag situations or symptoms that might lead you to start to engage in safety behaviours again;
- challenge a thought that the return of some anxiety must mean your panic disorder has returned;

- put into place strategies to prevent a lapse becoming a relapse;

- and know where to get help and support in the future should you need it.

My early warning signs

The first step in thinking about the future and dealing with any setbacks is to make a mental note of the things you might notice if your panic attacks begin to take hold. You may want to put this to the back of your mind but please try to spend some time thinking about it. These are the things that may indicate problems are starting to come back in the future. If you notice them and take early action, this can allow you to get on top of them before they begin to have an impact on your life.

Use Worksheet 21 to make a list of the things you think you are likely to experience as the first signs of problems recurring. Think back to a time when your panic disorder was first developing. Make a note of the changes you noticed in the following areas:

- Your *emotions*
- *Body sensations*
- Patterns in your *thinking*
- Your *behaviours*: what you did more or less of (make sure you think about safety behaviours, including escape and avoidance)

Having this list will help you spot early warning signs.

Often, other people can start to see change before we notice it ourselves. They can have some helpful observations. Perhaps they noticed you were starting to become more concerned about your health or that you had started to avoid going to some places by yourself. It might be you were doing more negative things to help you cope (e.g., using alcohol). It may be you started to need help for some things you used to do on your own. They might remember you saying you couldn't do some things or made excuses not to go places. Perhaps they noticed you were panicky in certain situations or seemingly out of the blue. It might be you began to say you were experiencing anxiety. Maybe they noticed you wouldn't go anywhere without something that made you feel safe (e.g., a bottle of water). Perhaps you became more tense or irritable more generally. Add these to your early warning signs in Worksheet 21.

If you notice red flags are creeping back into your life, this is a good indicator you need to take action. Use the techniques from Section 3 in the same way you did before. If you catch it early, it should be reasonably straightforward to regain the progress you previously made.

How things have improved since the start of this book

Reflecting on what you have achieved is an important part of relapse management. Some of the improvements you have noticed since starting work on your panic attacks might be linked to your symptoms (emotions, body sensations, thoughts and behaviours), and importantly, your lifestyle. Aspects of your lifestyle that might have changed include your:

- relationships and social life (with partner, family, work colleagues and friends);
- work life or ability to do other meaningful activities, such as voluntary work or being a carer for others;

- ability to do essential things outside the house like using public transport and shopping;
- and hobbies (solo ones such as going to the gym, as well as ones with others such as team sports or dancing).

Using Worksheet 22, make a list of any positive improvements in the following areas:

- **Symptoms** (emotions, body sensations, thoughts, and behaviours)
- **Relationships and social life**
- **Work or other meaningful activity**
- **Essential things outside the house**
- **Hobbies**

Re-rating your goals

In Section 1, you set some personal goals and now is the time to re-rate them (see Worksheet 5). If possible, try to rate your goals without looking at your previous ratings. Once you have rated them, review the progress you have made by comparing each of them with your first ratings, and any other ratings (you may have done them monthly). Sometimes, when change happens steadily, week by week, it is easy to lose track of all the progress you have made since the start, so this should help you get a good sense of how far you have come.

> ### Pause for reflection
> Take a moment to reflect on the progress you have made. Perhaps there are other things that have changed too. Perhaps you feel *happier* in your mood now you have got on top of your panic attacks.

What helped make improvements with your panic disorder?

What was it you did that helped you get on top of your panic disorder (and agoraphobia)? If you were able to go back in time and offer yourself some advice when you were just starting to work on your difficulties, what advice would that be? For example, perhaps you might suggest that you give things a go and drop safety behaviours despite the fear; it might be to be more patient with yourself within the testing experiments, or to make sure you dedicate more time to overcoming your panic attacks. Perhaps you might say it is important to generally approach rather than avoid. Make a note of this advice in Worksheet 23.

Now think about what advice you might give yourself if you became aware of a red flag situation which could lead to a lapse. Perhaps the advice would be quite similar to what you have just noted, or it might be completely different. For example, you might say it is important to enlist the help of a loved one again or to reinstate testing experiments if you were starting to avoid situations. Add this advice in Worksheet 23.

The wellbeing review

Another strategy you are likely to find helpful is scheduling regular wellbeing reviews. Ideally, mark a day in your calendar each month to prompt you to undertake a wellbeing review. Having a review day will help you spot red flags sooner and ensure you put into practice what you have learned in the book. Here is a structure to think through during your wellbeing review. It should take around twenty to thirty minutes. It is an opportunity to stop, think, and reflect on how you are doing and make any necessary changes at an early stage if needed. Perhaps you can set some dates in your calendar and have a reminder on your phone. Use the following questions for your wellbeing reviews in Worksheet 24.

My wellbeing review

Review date:

- *What have your panic-related symptoms been like over the last month?*
- *Reading through your red flags list, have you had any experiences that have concerned you?*

> - *Do you need to take any action now to keep on top of your panic attacks?*
> - *If so, what will be helpful to use from your toolkit?*
> - *What do you need to do and when are you going to do it?*
>
> The date of my next review is:

Is there anything else that you would like to work on?

Sometimes there are other areas in life people would like to see change in. These might be goals you set at the start of the book that you would like to work on further or perhaps new things you would now like to do. Some of your goals may not be completely met yet. Are there any difficulties that are getting in the way if this is the case? It is worth noting these down so you can remember them for later.

For the moment, it is probably best that you simply focus on maintaining the progress you have made so far. Once you have found you have maintained progress for a few months this is a good time to return to any other outstanding goals. Depending on what problems remain, it may be you can apply the strategies described in Section 3 to allow you to make progress. Or you may wish to use another book from the How to Beat series such as *How to Beat Agoraphobia* or *How to Beat Depression and Persistent Low Mood*. The other books in the series are structured very similarly to this one but focus on other problems. If you have managed to use this book, you should cope very well with the others in the series should you need them.

If you are being supported by a healthcare professional, they should be able to help you decide on how to move forward. Using Worksheet 25, take a moment to consider your answers to the following questions.

Issue(s) to work on in the future

- *What do you still want to work on?*

- *At this point, do you have any ideas how you will do this?*

- *When do you plan to do it (perhaps add in a reminder on your calendar for six months' time)?*

- *Are there any things that might get in the way of you working on this, and how might you overcome these?*

Relapse management top tips

Here are some top tips to help you use your toolkit to stay well:

1. The best way to prevent a lapse is to keep applying the skills you learned in Section 3 to maintain confidence. Remember the driving example? Just because you have passed your test doesn't mean you won't keep learning and building your confidence over time. Perhaps, every so often, try to do new things that create some anxiety (push the wall!). Use the principles you learned to tackle any anxiety or panic-related symptoms as needed.

2. Know your red flags. Watch out for times when you feel more stressed or when there is a lot of change in your life. If you have shared your red flags with others, they may be able to notice early negative changes in your symptoms.

3. Complete a wellbeing review even if you have been feeling well. It will remind you to keep going with what has been successful.

4. Check you haven't crept back into a panic cycle. If that has happened, think about how you can apply strategies from Section 3 to get back on top of your panic disorder.

5. Try not to be self-critical. Everyone is likely to experience setbacks at times. These are the body's natural response to situations that feel threatening (remember the body's alarm system). Focus on what you need to do to stop a lapse from becoming a relapse.

6. The thought of having to focus on using the strategies you learned again can feel a little disheartening. Try to focus on how effective it was for you before in addressing your difficulties. If it worked for you before, it is very likely to work again.

7. Use your toolkit as often as you need to and remember to carry out your wellbeing reviews. These don't have to be monthly. You may want to make them more frequent at first or if you have a setback. When you feel more confident in maintaining your progress, you can space the reviews out again.

Getting further help if you need it

Sometimes, despite your best efforts, you may still feel you require additional help. Knowing where and how to get help is an important final component of your toolkit. There are some organisations that may be able to support you listed in the *Further resources* section at the back of the book.

Now might also be a good time to think about some of the people around you who can form part of your 'wellbeing team'. Think of people around you who you trust and who can support you. Could you share your toolkit with them so they can help you watch out for red flags? Having read your toolkit, they will be aware of what you might need in order to feel better. Perhaps they can prompt you to access that? Make a note of the name of anyone you think would be a good supporter in that role.

Your doctor will usually be a key figure in your support plan. You may have been seeing your doctor or another healthcare professional periodically while you've been working through this book. If you need support, remember that your doctor is there to offer medical advice. They should also be able to refer you to another healthcare professional if needed.

Finally, make a note of any organisations you may want to contact should you need support from the

Further resources section at the back of this book. You can contact them when you are well and at your best, just so you are sure they are the right people to contact if you are experiencing difficulties.

Congratulations!

You've come a long way to reach this point, and it is fantastic you have managed to stay with the book. Take a moment to think about the progress you've made towards your goals. The journey may not have been straightforward, and you will have had to face your fears head on, which is never easy. The progress you have made is down to *you*! This book has just provided you with some tools to allow you to help yourself. Be proud of what you have achieved. Perhaps you can apply some of these principles to other areas of your life to help you to achieve other goals. In life, generally speaking, approaching is a much better strategy to solving problems than avoiding.

This relapse management section will help you keep hold of this progress. It will alert you when to put the necessary tools back into action if that situation arises. This book will always be here if you need it again.

In the next section, we return to Friya and Darius's stories. They will tell us how they used CBT self-help to get on top of their panic attacks. Some people write down their own story in the way Friya and Darius have told theirs. This acts as a reminder of what they have achieved. Others might write a short letter to themselves to celebrate their progress. Perhaps you could write your story after reading Friya and Darius's. You could write it as if it were a letter to yourself in the future, rather like a time capsule. Pieces of writing like this can also be added to your relapse management toolkit if you wish. You can re-read them as part of your wellbeing reviews, adding to them every so often as needed.

You should now have all the tools you need to keep your panic disorder (and agoraphobia) in check in the future. I wish you well.

Section 5

RECOVERY STORIES

Friya's story

Friya is a thirty-one-year-old single woman who lives with her son Beau, aged two. Her main difficulty is her fear of having a heart attack, particularly when alone. She's had panic disorder for seven years. Here is her recovery story.

'My panic disorder started with a panic attack when at home alone. I had been out earlier that day with friends in a café. We hadn't seen each other for ages so stayed there drinking several cups of coffee. I usually only have one cup of coffee when I get up, so this was unusual for me. Later when I was sitting watching TV, I noticed my heart was pounding. It seemed odd to me especially as I was in a happy mood having seen old friends earlier and I was sitting relaxing. I started focusing on my heartbeat, which seemed unusually fast. I then started feeling short of breath, I was sweating, I had chest pain, and I was trembling. I was terrified I was about to have a heart attack!

'That was my first panic attack (although I didn't learn that's what it was until later). I was so scared something so horrible could just come out of the blue, I thought I was going to die! I lay down and tried to control my breathing and within a few minutes the symptoms passed but it really shook me, and I was concerned there was something wrong with my heart so went to my doctor who said she thought I'd had a panic attack. She said it was probably a one-off because of the caffeine but to come back if I had any more similar episodes. I was not altogether convinced so I started regularly focusing on my heart to monitor for any discomfort or pain. I was really scared it would happen again when I was on my own and nobody would be there to help me.

'After that, I continued having the occasional panic attack when I was on my own. It was usually after I noticed a twinge in my heart and my chest would start to feel tight. At that point it felt like the panic attacks came out of the blue for no reason. Each time I would lie down and take deep breaths to get my breathing under control. The fact the first panic attack was not just a one-off like the doctor suggested made me worry there was something seriously wrong with my heart. So I went back to the doctor, and she conducted more thorough tests, but they were all clear, so she said there was definitely nothing wrong with my heart.

'I continued having panic attacks at home and it was after Beau was born my panic attacks worsened. One day when I was in the car, I had a panic attack while driving. I was able to pull over and put my seat back to allow me to do my deep breathing. After a few minutes, the symptoms passed, and I was able to drive home but I was left shaken by the whole thing. When I got back to work after maternity leave, I had a panic attack at work when I was in the office on my own. It was at this point it felt like the panic attacks could happen pretty much anywhere, especially when I was on my own when they seemed to come out of the blue for no reason and there was nobody there to help me.

'It started to feel like panic attacks were taking over my life. I stopped doing high-intensity exercise at the gym as I feared it was putting excess strain on my heart. Occasionally I would wake up in the middle of a panic attack, which was particularly frightening and convinced me that there must be something wrong with my heart. I became worried it would stop me being able to look after Beau.

'A further appointment with my doctor led to a diagnosis of panic disorder and I was offered some advice on how to overcome it including the offer of a referral to someone for support. I really wasn't sure about seeing someone at first, so I decided to try to address the problem myself using self-help. I agreed I would go back if I continued to have problems so that she could refer me for professional help. I wasn't sure how I would get on with working on a problem I'd had for seven years by myself but thought I would give it a go.

'So, I started reading up about panic disorder and could see I fitted the criteria! That was reassuring in some ways, as sometimes I felt so alone with it. It also helped explain why the problem had become worse over the years as it crept into various areas of my life. I took a good hard look at how the panic attacks had affected my life over the years and set myself some goals. I enlisted the help of my close friend Jen, and I am not sure I could have done it without her.

'I found the panic cycle incredibly useful in helping me understand what happens in panic attacks.

I started with my most recent panic attack then used it for several more and I was able to see a pattern emerge. I also did a panic cycle for my first ever panic attack. I cannot exaggerate how helpful it was to see how the cycle made complete sense. But I was still anxious! I found the discovery experiments really interesting and helpful. They helped make sense of my body sensations and how my interpretation, or should I say misinterpretation, of them added to my feelings of panic. Then when I added in my safety behaviours of deep breathing and lying down it made even more sense.

'There was a lot of information to take in to understand what happens in a panic attack and deep down I still feared there must be something wrong with my heart. Reading about the body's alarm system really made sense as did looking at the body and why some sensations happen when we are anxious. This helped shake my thoughts a bit, so I no longer believed 100% there was something wrong with my heart. Learning what happens in a heart attack was a big turning point for me as my body sensations fell into the non-cardiac chest pain category. That was an 'aha moment' for me in shaking up my thoughts about being at risk of having a heart attack.

'I kept diaries of my panic attacks and tried out various discovery experiments before doing testing experiments. They really helped build my confidence and it became clear I needed to address my fear of having a weak heart. Jen helped me with the first testing experiment of running up and down stairs. We ended up having a bit of a laugh about it. We must have looked ridiculous running up and down stairs for five minutes. We were almost crawling by the end of it. What happened though was central to me shifting my thought that something bad would happen in a panic attack and that my prediction of having a heart attack within a minute was shown to be untrue. This helped me in being more confident to go for a run with Jen the next day then do these things on my own without my safety behaviours during or after!

'I make it sound super easy, but it wasn't all plain sailing as I did hit a couple of stumbling blocks along the way. I had been doing really well with the testing experiments and dropping safety behaviours and was even back at the gym doing high-intensity exercise classes but one day when I was working from home and Beau was at nursery, I had a panic attack out of the blue. It really threw me as I hadn't had one for a while and there was no obvious trigger (at first). I worried I was back to square one and that all the hard work I had put into addressing my panic attacks had been for nothing. But I knew from what I had learned that panic attacks do not simply come out of the blue. So, I dug out a panic cycle and worked through it to make sense of what happened. I had been out the night before for a boozy evening with friends and had slept badly, getting up and down to the loo and having a less restful night than usual. I was tired the next morning and feeling a bit under the weather. As I was so tired, I had a couple of extra cups of coffee to get me going. Of course, this was a bad idea, and I noticed my heart rate being quicker than usual later. It wasn't until I sat down and worked through the panic cycle that it all made sense. Note to self not to have too boozy a night before a workday and not to try to wake myself up with too much coffee! It was good to be able to make sense of the recent panic attack, so it felt less significant in terms of my progress.

'My other blip was when I read about a footballer dying suddenly of a heart attack. He was only twenty-four. It was shocking. I didn't deal with it well and had a temporary re-emergence of chest pain and other panic symptoms. I was concerned that maybe I did have a weak heart, and the same thing could happen to me. Again, I sat down and tried to make sense of it. That helped, and I was soon back to normal, but it showed me that something linking to my panic experiences could be quite triggering. I added this to my red flags list.

'I carried on with the testing experiments and now I truly feel like I have conquered my panic disorder. Everything I did, from the panic cycle to learning about panic attacks and trying out the discovery exercises, helped prepare me for the testing experiments. The apprentice story helped me recognise I had to be brave and test out whether my wall would fall down by letting go of my safety behaviours. It stayed standing! What a wonderful feeling that is. Jen helped me with my relapse management plan and to think through my red flags. So far so good – it's been six months now since my last panic attack. I have my life back!'

Darius's story

Darius is forty-two and lives with his partner of ten years, Jasmine. He has been living with panic disorder for fifteen years which progressed to agoraphobia within a year of his first panic attack. His main difficulty is leaving the house unaccompanied for fear of collapsing.

'I'd had panic disorder and agoraphobia for a long time before I felt like I really had to do something about it. My problems with panic had started at work fifteen years ago and it escalated from there to the point where my life was incredibly restricted. I was working from home and struggled to go anywhere without Jasmine by my side in case I collapsed. I had stopped having sex because the sensations of dizziness and light-headedness frightened me. This led to tension in our relationship. Covid-19 took a bit of pressure off me as there was no expectation of anyone going into the office. But as restrictions eased, I was under pressure again to return to the workplace for a minimum of once a month but preferably at least once a week. I had various medical checks, and the doctors all said there was nothing wrong with me, but I couldn't shake it off.

'As I was approaching my forty-second birthday I took stock of my life. I'd been living with panic disorder for fifteen years, I had agoraphobia, I was too frightened to have sex with my partner, and I was feeling low in mood. Things couldn't get much worse. I was also under a great deal of pressure to return to the office, and I felt concerned I would lose my job if I didn't get myself in there. I felt like everything was closing in on me and I was struggling to see a way forward. Losing my job would have massive implications for our lives including being able to afford the roof over our heads, especially since our mortgage rate had gone up in recent months. I was feeling really down on myself about the whole thing. My doctor offered me some antidepressants which I took for a while, but I knew it was the panic attacks that were really the nub of the problem as the depression came second, third really after the agoraphobia so I didn't take them for long.

'As my birthday got closer, I just got to thinking, is this what the rest of my life is going to look like? I really didn't want that to be the case. I missed the freedom to go where I wanted when I wanted even though it was hard to remember a more carefree life as it seemed so long ago. I started researching panic disorder on the internet and found lots of useful information. CBT seemed to be a recurring theme for the approach that was most likely to help. I also talked to Jasmine about the reasons I was avoiding having sex which helped. She had suspected that was the case.

'Although my whole life seemed restricted by my panic disorder and agoraphobia, I managed to narrow down my goals to a few that would be a clear indicator it was no longer a problem and I was free to live my life including going into work once a week, using the bus, and having sex with Jasmine again.

'I was a bit sceptical about the panic cycle but sure enough, every panic attack I went through the cycle with (and I did a fair few including my first one) all seemed to fit into place and made sense. I was also able to do some of the discovery and testing experiments and they were incredibly powerful. I found the paired words task particularly helpful and the pink rabbit one made me laugh as the bloomin' thing kept on coming to mind throughout the five minutes. My agoraphobic anxieties lessened as I did more exercises that chipped away at my understanding of what was wrong with me. Jasmine helped me with the over-breathing exercise which was an important learning point. I didn't do it quite right at first as I was tensing my leg muscles while doing the over-breathing. So, I did it again and didn't tense my legs the second time which I knew very well was one of my safety behaviours. It was harder doing it the second time, but I learned more doing it correctly! The blurred vision exercises also helped challenge my thinking around dizziness, as did the leg muscle tensing exercise. Jasmine was cheering me on from the kitchen window while I walked up and down the garden. Goodness knows what the neighbours thought if they were looking out their windows, I didn't dare look up!

'All these exercises helped me to learn more about my panic attacks and to see my problem was down to my interpretation of body sensations rather than there being something wrong. Jasmine helped me with the testing experiments. I found them really tough at first, even with her help, and I lost my way for a bit and could feel the problems returning. After a while I went back to the doctor and asked to be referred for help. I saw a lovely therapist who guided me on how to get the most out of the testing experiments as well as cheering me on.

'If I could give one piece of advice to someone else with panic disorder and agoraphobia, I would tell them to do their utmost to work on the problem earlier rather than later. I lived a lot of years feeling desperately unhappy because of how panic attacks restricted my life. It is not easy to do but it is better than living with it day in day out; that was miserable. My mood improved and I feel genuinely happy with my life now. If I am allowed to give another piece of advice it would be not to be frightened of asking for more support. The help from the therapist really was the turning point in me being able to finally reclaim my life.'

My red flags

Stopping having sex

Being reluctant to go into the office

Avoiding using the bus

Not going places without Jasmine, such as the shops

My wellbeing review

Review date: 26th October

What have your symptoms been like over the last month?

Pretty good. I've had the odd time when I have felt a bit anxious, but I tried out a few new things like going to the cinema complex on my own so perhaps it's not surprising. I've not avoided doing anything, which I am pleased about.

Reading through your red flags list, have you had any experiences that have concerned you?

Not really. I did have an urge to stay at home last week rather than go into the office, but I reminded myself that I shouldn't just stay in because it's windy and cold outside. We are approaching winter so it is going to be like this for a while and I cannot risk a relapse by making excuses to stay at home. I went to the office by bus, and it was fine. I know I need to push myself when the weather is bad, or I can't be bothered. That's probably like a lot of people and it's normal for me. Even before my panic disorder I didn't like going out in bad weather. Besides, I had committed to going into the office every Wednesday and knowing that colleagues expected to see me helped.

Do you need to take any action now to keep on top of your panic attacks?

Not this month. I'm doing stuff: going to work, going to the shops, getting the bus.

And, I have been having sex regularly which has been great for my relationship with Jasmine — we feel closer.

If so, what will be helpful to use from your toolkit?

Not necessary. I just need to keep on doing what I'm doing but be mindful of my red flags and keep an eye out for anything important. Jasmine is well aware of my red flags too and will let me know if she notices anything.

What do you need to do and when are you going to do it?

I need to do more of the same but we're also planning a trip to London so although Jasmine and I will be together, I am going to push myself to get on the Underground alone and separate from her a bit in unfamiliar places a couple of times too.

The date of my next review is: 16th November

WORKBOOK

Worksheet 1

List of common panic disorder symptoms

Symptoms	Tick if this applies to you
Palpitations, heart pounding/racing	
Sweating	
Trembling or shaking	
Shortness of breath or the feeling of being smothered	
Choking sensations	
Chest pain	
Nausea	
Tummy upset or discomfort	
Dizziness, light-headedness, feeling unsteady or faint	
Chills or heat sensations	
Numbness or tingling	
Feelings of unreality or like you are detached from yourself	
Fear of losing control or 'going mad'	
Fear that you are going to die	

Worksheet 2

Graph for plotting PDSS scores

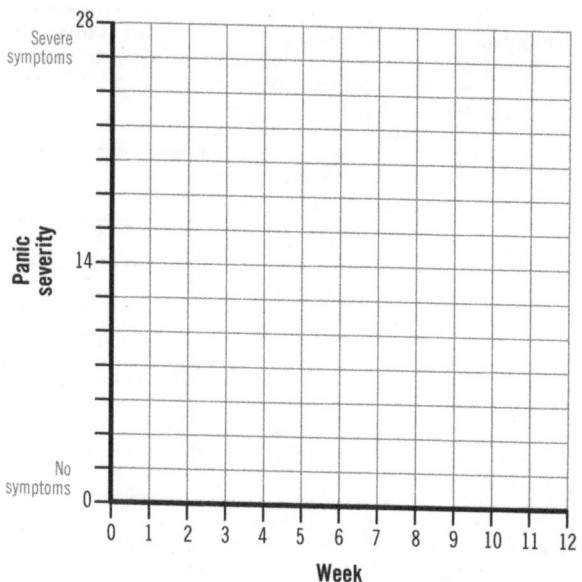

Worksheet 3

Agoraphobia problem areas

Problem area	Situation	Tick if this applies to you
Transport such as:	Being a passenger in a taxi	
	Using the bus or tram	
	Travelling by train	
	Using the underground	
	Sailing on ships	
	Travelling by aeroplane	
Open spaces such as:	Car parks	
	Marketplaces	
Enclosed spaces such as:	Shops	
	Supermarkets	
	Department stores	
	Theatres	
	Cinemas	
Standing in a queue		
Being in a crowd		
Being away from home alone		

Worksheet 4

Making change happen – limitations of living with panic disorder

List all the ways your panic attacks have limited your life to date

How might this problem impact your life in future if it remains the same or worsens?

How will it interfere with you achieving your life goals?

What have you had to sacrifice for this problem?

What would your life look like if you woke up tomorrow and you no longer experienced regular panic attacks? What would be different?

What do you need to put in place to give you the best chance of completing this self-help?

Worksheet 5

My goals for beating my panic disorder

Goal 1: ....

....

....

I can do this now   (Today's date __/__/__)
(circle a number):

0	1	2	3	4	5	6
Not at all		Occasionally		Often		Any time

One month re-rating   (date __/__/__)
(circle a number):

0	1	2	3	4	5	6
Not at all		Occasionally		Often		Any time

Two month re-rating   (date __/__/__)
(circle a number):

0	1	2	3	4	5	6
Not at all		Occasionally		Often		Any time

Three month re-rating   (date __/__/__)
(circle a number):

0	1	2	3	4	5	6
Not at all		Occasionally		Often		Any time

Goal 2: ....

....

....

I can do this now (Today's date __/__/__)
(circle a number):

0	1	2	3	4	5	6
Not at all		Occasionally		Often		Any time

One month re-rating (date __/__/__)
(circle a number):

0	1	2	3	4	5	6
Not at all		Occasionally		Often		Any time

Two month re-rating (date __/__/__)
(circle a number):

0	1	2	3	4	5	6
Not at all		Occasionally		Often		Any time

Three month re-rating (date __/__/__)
(circle a number):

0	1	2	3	4	5	6
Not at all		Occasionally		Often		Any time

Goal 3: ....

....

....

I can do this now (Today's date __/__/__)
(circle a number):

0   1   2   3   4   5   6
Not at all   Occasionally   Often   Any time

One month re-rating (date __/__/__)
(circle a number):

0   1   2   3   4   5   6
Not at all   Occasionally   Often   Any time

Two month re-rating (date __/__/__)
(circle a number):

0   1   2   3   4   5   6
Not at all   Occasionally   Often   Any time

Three month re-rating (date __/__/__)
(circle a number):

0   1   2   3   4   5   6
Not at all   Occasionally   Often   Any time

Worksheet 6

My panic cycle

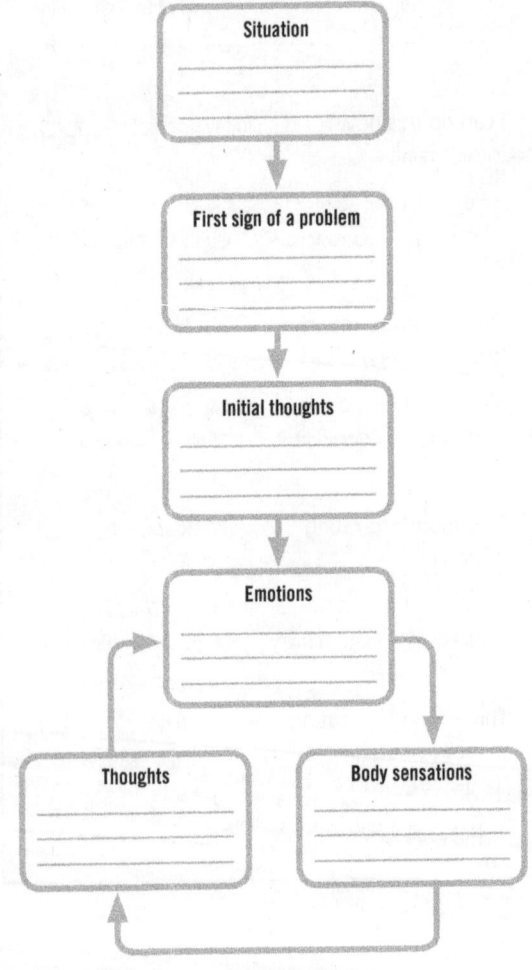

Worksheet 7

My safety behaviours

What I do to stop myself from having panic attacks (e.g. avoid some situations – list them; escape situations if feeling uneasy; carry things like tablets or a water bottle; ensure I'm accompanied).

What I do during a panic attack to help me feel better (e.g. distraction; holding onto something; sitting/lying down; standing still/tensing muscles; moving slowly; controlling thoughts; taking medication/alcohol; controlling breathing; relaxation).

Worksheet 8
Panic diary

Date	Situation you were in when the panic attack happened and first symptom you noticed	Level of severity of panic attack (0–100 with 100 being the most severe it could be)	Main body sensations	How you interpreted the body sensations (0–100 where 0 = did not believe it to 100 = completely believed the thought)	Alternative explanation and re-rate your negative interpretation of body sensations (0–100 where 0 = did not believe it to 100 = completely believed the alternative explanation)

Worksheet 9
Weekly review form

Date:

My PDSS score this week:

Number of panic attacks this week:

Severity of panic attacks this week (use a 0–100 scale with 100 being the most severe it could be):

What I have learned this week about my panic attacks including any changes in thought about them:

Worksheet 10

Discovery experiment 1 – understanding the role of thoughts and images in panic attacks (pink rabbit experiment)

For the next couple of minutes DO NOT think about a pink rabbit with big floppy ears, a white fluffy tail, and a twitchy nose with extra-long whiskers.

Once you have done that, do whatever you can to get rid of the pink rabbit. While making sure you are not thinking about our outsized pink rabbit, say out loud whatever is going through your mind, it really doesn't matter what you say. If the rabbit does come to mind, try to push it away and pop a dot below every time it pops into mind.

Once the two minutes is up, answer the following questions:

1. How often did you think about the rabbit?
2. What can we make of this?
3. How does it relate to trying to push thoughts out of your mind during a panic attack?
4. Might it be that trying to push distressing thoughts out of your mind is having the opposite effect and if so, could you do something different next time?

What have you learned from this exercise?

Rate your level of belief in your catastrophic thought (from 0 = 'I don't believe it at all' to 100 = 'I believe it completely'):

Before exercise:

After exercise:

Worksheet 11

Discovery experiment 2 – what makes me think something bad will happen?

Brief description of recent panic attack	Level of severity of panic attack (0–100)	Main body sensations	What I thought was going to happen	My evidence for my catastrophic thought being true

What have you learned from this exercise?

Rate your level of belief in your catastrophic thought (from 0 = 'I don't believe it at all' to 100 = 'I believe it completely'):

Before exercise:

After exercise:

Worksheet 12

Discovery experiment 3 – understanding the nature of anxiety (body sensations in different mood states)

Body sensations when I am angry	Body sensations when I am excited	Body sensations when I am having a panic attack

What are the similarities across the three sets of body sensations?

What are the differences across the three sets of body sensations?

What have you learned from this exercise?

Rate your level of belief in your catastrophic thought (from 0 = "I don't believe it at all" to 100 = "I believe it completely"):

Before exercise:

After exercise:

Worksheet 13

Discovery experiment 4 – focus of attention

Please set aside ten minutes for this exercise. Close your eyes for a couple of minutes and scan your body to notice as many sensations as you can. Spend this time really focusing on what is going on in your body, head to toe. Once you have done that, open your eyes and pay attention to something near you, perhaps a painting, a bookshelf or a fruit bowl (anything that has some detail) and describe it in great detail out loud.

When you stop, ask yourself the following questions:

1. When you had your eyes closed and you were focusing on what was happening in your body, how strong were the sensations?

2. When you had your eyes open and were describing something near you in great detail, what happened to your body sensations?

3. If the sensations decreased or you did not notice them after a while when looking at something in detail, what does that tell you about the power of focusing your attention on something external rather than focusing on what is happening to you internally?

What have you learned from this exercise?

Rate your level of belief in your catastrophic thought (from 0 = 'I don't believe it at all' to 100 = 'I believe it completely'):
Before exercise:
After exercise:

Worksheet 14

Discovery experiment 5 – pairs of words

What did you notice in your body when you were reading out the words?

If you experienced body sensations, how similar were they to what you experience at the start of a panic attack?

Did you get any mental images when you went through certain words?

Which words?

Were some words harder than others to read?

If you answered yes to the last question, what do you make of that?

If you think of your feared catastrophe, how possible would it be that reading or thinking about a word could bring that on?

What have you learned from this exercise?

Rate your level of belief in your catastrophic thought (from 0 = 'I don't believe it at all' to 100 = 'I believe it completely'):

Before exercise:

After exercise:

Worksheet 15

Discovery experiment for specific body sensations – 1. Fainting (symptoms contrast table for fainting versus panic attack)

Symptoms when I fainted	Symptoms when I panic

What have you learned from this exercise?

Rate your level of belief in your catastrophic thought (from 0 = 'I don't believe it at all' to 100 = 'I believe it completely'):

Before exercise:

After exercise:

Worksheet 16

Discovery experiments

Use for:

Specific body sensations – 2. Collapsing

Specific body sensations – 3. Stopping breathing

Specific body sensations – 5. Going insane or losing consciousness

Specific body sensations – 6. Choking

What you did
Sensations you experienced
What have you learned from this exercise?
Rate your level of belief in your catastrophic thought (from 0 = 'I don't believe it at all' to 100 = 'I believe it completely'): Before exercise: After exercise:

Worksheet 17

Discovery experiment for specific body sensations – 4. Having a heart attack

Symptoms of pain experienced in a panic attack:
Symptoms of pain experienced in heart disease:
What have you learned from this exercise?
Rate your level of belief in your catastrophic thought (from 0 = 'I don't believe it at all' to 100 = 'I believe it completely'): Before exercise: After exercise:

Worksheet 18

Consolidating learning from discovery experiments

List all the evidence you have collected so far that contradicts your worst fears about your panic-related sensations and safety behaviours and how they fit with the CBT model of panic.

What do you make of the evidence you have collected so far?

What have you learned from this exercise?

Rate your level of belief in your catastrophic thought (from 0 = 'I don't believe it at all' to 100 = 'I believe it completely'):

Before exercise:

After exercise:

Worksheet 19

Testing experiment diary

Testing experiment diary
Date:
Preparation for experiment
My catastrophic panic thought: **Strength of conviction (0–100%):**
Ideas for experiment to test the catastrophic panic thought (circle the best one). Remember it is vital you do not engage in any safety behaviours so include this in your ideas. 1. 2. 3. 4.
Specific predictions about what will happen in this experiment, how you will know if your prediction is true, and your strength of conviction (0–100%). **Prediction:**   **How I will know if my prediction is true:**   **Strength of conviction (0–100%):**

Post-experiment analysis

Describe the experiment you carried out and whether you engaged in any safety behaviours:

Did your prediction come true?

Re-rate your conviction in your original thought:

What have you learned from the experiment and how likely do you think it is that your original prediction will happen sometime in the future?

What else can you do to test your original prediction?

Worksheet 20
Avoidance list

This is a list of situations and places that you tend to avoid on your own and if possible. Categorise them from moderately difficult to extremely difficult/impossible.

Moderately difficult

Extremely difficult

Worksheet 21

Early warning signs/red flags

Make a list of the things you think you are likely to experience as the first signs of problems recurring. Think back to a time when your panic disorder was first developing. Make a note of the changes you noticed in the following areas:

Your emotions	
Body sensations	
Patterns of your thinking	
Your behaviours: what you did more or less of (make sure you think about safety behaviours such as escape and avoidance)	

Worksheet 22

Positive improvements

List any positive improvements in the following areas:

Symptoms (emotions, body sensations, thoughts and behaviours)	
Relationships and social life	
Work or other meaningful activity	
Essential things outside the house	
Hobbies	

Worksheet 23

What helped make improvements with your panic disorder?

What was it you did that helped you get on top of your panic disorder (and agoraphobia)?

If you were able to go back in time and offer yourself some advice when you were just starting to work on your difficulties, what advice would that be?

What advice might you give yourself if you became aware of a red flag situation which could lead to a lapse?

Worksheet 24

My wellbeing review

Review date:
What have your panic-related symptoms been like over the last month?
Reading through your red flags list, have you had any experiences that have concerned you?
Do you need to take any action now to keep on top of your panic attacks?

Workbook 231

If so, what will be helpful to use from your toolkit?

What do you need to do and when are you going to do it?

The date of my next review is:

Worksheet 25

Issues to work on in the future

What do you still want to work on?

At this point, do you have any ideas how you will do this?

When do you plan to do it (perhaps add in a reminder on your calendar for six months' time)?

Are there any things that might get in the way of you working on this, and how might you overcome these?

FURTHER RESOURCES

UK

The National Health Service (in the UK)

The UK NHS website has a summary of useful information about panic disorder and agoraphobia. The relevant links are:

www.nhs.uk/conditions/panicdisorder

www.nhs.uk/conditions/agoraphobia

www.nhs.uk/mental-health/conditions/clinical-depression/overview

The website also has details of other anxiety conditions. Reading through these should help you confirm whether your difficulties are symptoms of panic disorder (rather than a different anxiety condition). The following page will also allow you to determine whether you might be experiencing another anxiety condition:

www.nhs.uk/common-health-questions/lifestyle/do-i-have-an-anxiety-disorder

You can find a psychological treatment service in England via this page: www.nhs.uk/service-search/mental-health/find-an-NHS-talking-therapies-service

Remember that your doctor will be able to discuss these things with you as well as support you in your CBT self-help and refer you to a psychological practitioner if appropriate. Remember to keep you doctor informed of all the treatments you are involved in and all the healthcare professionals you are in contact with.

Private sector

If you would like to find a private CBT therapist (who will charge a fee for each session) you can use this website: babcp.com/CBTRegister/Search#

Support agencies

If you have suicidal thoughts and are planning to act on those thoughts, please access support from a crisis team which can be accessed in the UK through your GP, your local accident and emergency department or the police.

NHS 111 provides urgent care, advice and mental health support 24 hours a day.

Phone: 111

Website: www.111.nhs.uk

Samaritans is a voluntary organisation providing support to people in distress 24 hours a day.

Phone: 116 123

Email: jo@samaritans.org

Website: www.samaritans.org

Shout is a free, confidential text messaging service offering support for anyone who is struggling to cope 24 hours a day.

Text: Shout to 85258

Website: www.giveusashout.org

Breathing Space (Scotland) provides a free support service for anyone in Scotland over 16 who is experiencing low mood, depression or anxiety. As well as a phone service, they offer live webchat from Monday to Friday 6pm to 2am and Saturday and Sunday 4pm to 12am.

Phone: 0800 83 85 87 (24 hours at weekends and 6pm to 2am weekdays)

Website: www.breathingspace.scot

CALM (Campaign Against Living Miserably) is a charity that offers a helpline and live chat for anyone over 15 every day from 5pm to 12am.

Phone: 0800 58 58 58

Website: www.thecalmzone.net

Lifeline (Northern Ireland) is a 24-hour crisis helpline service for people in Northern Ireland who are experiencing distress.

Phone: 0808 808 8000

Website: www.lifelinehelpline.info

Mind is a charity providing advice and support to people experiencing mental health difficulties (Monday to Friday, 9am to 5pm).

Phone: 0208 215 2243

Email: info@mind.org.uk

Website: www.mind.org.uk

SANELine is a national out-of-hours charity mental health helpline offering emotional support every day from 4pm to 10pm.

Phone: 0300 304 7000

Website: www.sane.or.uk

Australia

The Australian Government Department of Health, Disability and Ageing provides contact details for a variety of mental health support organisations.

Website: www.health.gov.au

Beyond Blue is a reliable source of free mental health information, advice and support.

Website: www.beyondblue.org.au

Mindspot offers free online and telephone support including psychological assessment and evidence-based treatments.

Website: www.mindspot.org.au

Canada

The Centre for Addiction and Mental Health (CAMH) is Canada's largest mental health teaching hospital. They have a webpage dedicated to panic disorder.

Website: www.camh.ca/en/health-info/mental-illness-and-addiction-index/panic-disorder

Ontario Structured Psychotherapy OSP Program

CAMH coordinates the OSP for the Toronto region. The programme is free and offers short-term CBT providing practical and goal-oriented support.

Website: www.camh.ca/en/patients-and-families/programs-and-services/ontario-structured-psychotherapy-osp-program

New Zealand

The Mental Health Foundation provides information and resources for all mental health conditions including panic disorder and includes links to helplines and local mental health services.

Website: mentalhealth.org.nz/conditions/condition/panic-disorder#treatment-options

Republic of Ireland

Mental Health Ireland aims to promote and enhance mental health, wellbeing and recovery. They provide information on how to contact mental health services and how to access helplines.

Website: www.mentalhealthireland.ie/mental-health-services

Website: www.mentalhealthireland.ie/get-support

USA

The US Centers for Disease Control and Prevention provides information on mental health problems and provides information on how to get help.

Website: www.cdc.gov/mental-health/about

The National Institute of Mental Health provides information about mental health conditions including panic disorder and provides information on how to get help.

Website: www.nimh.nih.gov/health/publications/panic-disorder-when-fear-overwhelms

ACKNOWLEDGEMENTS

I dedicate this book to my siblings: Kath, Irene, Ally and Jenny. I would like to thank Antony for his unwavering support while writing this book.

Thank you to Andrew McAleer, Editorial Director for Robinson Psychology, and Mark Papworth, Series Editor, for asking me to write this book and for their support throughout.

The CBT protocol for treating panic disorder by Professor David Clark was used to inform this book.

INDEX

Note: page numbers in **bold** refer to diagrams, page numbers in *italics* refer to information contained in tables and worksheets.

advice 14, 35, 172
agoraphobia 3–4, 6, 17, 24–5, 89
    and CBT self-help 20, 41, 43, 81, *200*
    definition 10–11
    diagnosis 11
    and goal-setting 41, 43
    problem areas *200*
    recurrent 83
    stand-alone 13
    symptoms 12–13
    see also panic disorder, agoraphobia as complication of
alcohol consumption 34, 168, 187
anger 59, 108–9, *110*
antidepressants 15
anxiety 5, 11, 33, 58–9, 69
    and body sensations 60–2, **63**, 64–5, 68, 99, 107–9, *110*, 111, 115, 119
    definition 4
    duration 5
    experience in agoraphobia 11, 12
    and fainting 119–20
    medication for 15
    normal levels of 6
    overcoming 83
    and panic attack
        maintenance factors **66**, 67–9, **70**, 71, 74, **78**, 79–80
    paralysing 33
    and phobias 17
    and recovery stories 185, 191, 193–4
    recurrent 83
    and relapse prevention 166, 168, 176
    and safety behaviours 74
    strategies to overcome 99, 107–9, *110*, 111, 115, 119–20, 143, 145–6, 150, 153, *214–15*
    and testing experiments 150, 153
    understanding the nature of 107–9, *110*, *214–15*
    and vicious cycles 68
anxiety disorders 2, 6, 10, 15–18
    and CBT 20
    prevalence 6

strategies to overcome 89
successful treatment of 83
see also agoraphobia; panic disorder
apprehension 4, 5
attention, focus of 111–14, 165, *216–17*
avoidance behaviours 10, 11, 16, 55, 82
and relapse management 166, 168
as safety behaviour 74, 75
testing experiments for 144–9, *145*
worksheet *226*

behaviours 48–9
during a panic attack 52–3, 56–7
and overcoming panic disorder 99, 101
and relapse prevention 168
benzodiazepines 15
blood pressure 119
body sensations 48–9, 52, 66, **91**
of anxiety 60–2, **63**, 64–5, 68, 99, 107–9, *110*, 111, 115, 119
during sleep 84
interpreting in a catastrophic way 19, 56, 59, 64–5, *65*, 69, **70**, 71–3, 84, *86–7*, 90, 92–3, 99–100, **100**, 102–3, 105–9, *110*, 111–34, *116–17*, **129**, 148–9, 151, 154, 156, 163, 165, 185, *211–23*
and maintenance of panic attacks **66**, 68, 69, **70**, 71–3
not listening to your 33

re-interpreting *86–7*, 92, 98–100, **100**, 133–4, 155–6, 165
reasons not to focus on in CBT self-help 98–101, **100**
recording in panic diaries 85, *86–7*
and relapse prevention 168
and safety behaviours 75
understanding 107–9, *110*, *214–15*
and vicious cycles 68

breathing
controlled 50–1, 52, 73–4, 77, **78**, 79, 99, 124, 138–9, *141*, 182–3, 185, 198
fear of stopping/shortness of 7, 50, 52–3, 64–5, *65*, 69, **70**, **78**, *110*, *116–17*, 118, 123–5, 138–9, *141*, 143–4, 182–3, *198*, 221
over-breathing ('hyperventilation') 56, *86*, 123–5, 151, 191–2
rapid **63**, *65*, 67, *121*, 151
when sleeping 84

caffeine 18–19, 34, 59, 181–2, 187
case examples 23, 49–58
Darius 49–50, 53–9, 75, 85, *86–7*, 108, 111–14, 119, 125, 144–8, *145*, 151, 153, 163, 179–80, 189–95
Friya 49–53, 57–60, 68–9, **70**, 75, 78–9, *78*, 106–7, 109, 111, 112–13, 125–7, 137–8, *137–9*, *140–1*, 151, 163, 179–80, 181–8

CBT self-help 3–4, 21–46, 49–58, 71–2, 81, 83
  and agoraphobia 20, 41, 43, 81, *200*
  getting going 24
  giving it your best shot 28–9, 38
  goals of 32–3, 41–6, 53, 57, 90, 95, 171, 174, 191, *203–5*
  and goods days/bad days 31–2
  and note-keeping 30–1
  and overcoming panic disorder 25
  and professional support 37–9
  putting what you learn into action 29–30
  setting time aside for 36
  top tips 27–36
  workbook 27, 197–232
  see also case examples; panic diaries; recovery stories; relapse prevention tool-kit; strategies to overcome panic disorder
change
  making it happen 40–1, *201–2*
  opportunities for 41
chest pain 5, 7, 50, 52, **63**, 68–9, **70**, 78, *110*, 126–7, 182, 185, 187
choking, fear of 7, 105, *116–17*, 118, 130, *198*, *221*
cognitive behavioural therapy (CBT) 2, 15, 19
  definition 20–1
  types of provision 20–1
  see also CBT self-help
collapse, fear of 11, 48, 54, 56, 59, **65**, 75, **86**, 105, 111–12, 115, *116–17*, 122, 125, *140*, 146–8, 163, 189, *221*
coping statements 149–50, 153

dangerous situations
  and anxiety 6
  bodily response to 62, **63**
  mistaking body sensations as dangerous 72–3, 84
'default settings', moving away from your 33
depression 18, 20, 39, 82
diazepam 15
discovery experiments 90, *91*, 92, 95–6, 101–32, 148–9, 153–5
  consolidating learning from 130–2, *223*
  and focus of attention 111–14, *216–17*
  and pairs of words 114–17, *116–17*, 191, *218–19*
  and recovery stories 185, 188, 191
  and the role of thoughts and images in panic attacks 103–5, 211, *211*
  and specific body sensations 118–27, *220–1*
  and understanding the nature of anxiety 107–9, *110*, *214–15*
  and understanding what makes you think something bad will happen 105–7, *212–13*
doctors 33–5, 37–9, 154, 178, 182–4
drug use 18–19

early warning signs 164, 166–9, 172–3, 176, 178, 187, 193–4, *227*
emotions 48–9, 52, 56, 59, **91**
    as panic attack maintenance factors **66**, 67, 69, **70**, 71–2, *78*
    and relapse prevention 168
    see also specific emotions
enclosed spaces, fear of 11, 12, 17, *200*
escape behaviours 74–5, *76*, 144, 168, *207*, *227*
excitement 108–9, *110*

fainting 7, 8–9, 56, 65, 68, 74, 81, *86*, 105, *116–17*, 118–23, *121*, 125, 146–7, 149, *198*, *220*
families 21, 35–6
fear
    catastrophic 11
    definition 4
    experience in agoraphobia 10, 11, 12
    experience in panic attacks 5, 13–14, 118
    experience in panic disorder 11
    of fear 6, 82
    and generalised anxiety disorder 17–18
    and phobias 10, 11, 12, 17
    and safety behaviours 74
    see also agoraphobia; *specific fears of panic disorder*
fight or flight response 60–2, **63**, 107
flash cards 149–50, 153
flashbacks 17
friends 21, 35–6

gender bias 6
generalisation 74

generalised anxiety disorder (GAD) 17–18
goals 32–3, 41–6, 53, 57, 90, 95, 191, *203–5*
    re-rating 171
    reviewing unmet 174
    SMART 42–3

healthcare professionals
    support from 21, 23, 28–9, 33–5, 37–9, 81, 153, 159, 161, 175, 178, 184
    see also doctors
heart attacks, fear of having 5, 8–9, 11, 50, 52, 65, 68–9, **70**, 73–4, **78**, 79, 105–7, 112, 115, *116–17*, 118, 125–7, 137–9, *140–1*, 146, 151, 163, 181–7, *222*
heart rate 7, 19, 51, 62, **63**, 64–5, *65*, 67–8, 137–8, 151, 187, *198*
hobbies 170, *228*
hopelessness 39, 164
hormonal changes 19

images, role in panic attacks 103–5, 211, *211*
insanity, fear of 9, 11, 62, 65, 68, 127–9, **129**, 142–3, *221*

lapses 163–7, 176, 177
life stresses 18, 162
lorazepam 15

medication for panic disorder 15
    side-effects 34–5

National Health Service (NHS) 2, 3
NHS Education for Scotland 3

NHS Expert Advisory Group
 for Talking Therapies for
 Anxiety and Depression 3
nightmares 17

open spaces, fear of 12, *200*
over-breathing
 ('hyperventilation') 56,
 86, 123–5, 151, 191–2

pain *see* chest pain
pairs of words (exercise) 114–17,
 116–17, 191
palpitations 7, 19, 64–5, *65*,
 198
panic, definition 4
panic attacks 1, 3, 4
 and agoraphobia 10, 11,
  19, 80–1
 bodily sensations of 61–2,
  63, **66**, 68
 and CBT self-help 23–30,
  32–3, 40–5, 50–7, *91*,
  92–103, 105–7, 109,
  110, 111–33, *116–17*,
  121, 136–7, 142–4, 148,
  153–4, 156–7, 159–63,
  165–7, 169, 171–2,
  174, 177, *211–13*, *218*,
  220, 222
 changing your thinking
  around 24
 definition 5
 and depression 18
 and diagnosing panic
  disorder 7
 duration 5
 early warning signs 84
 and emotions **66**, 67, 69,
  70, 71
 fear of/being scared of
  13–14, 16
 fear of the social
  consequences of 11
 fear of the symptom
  consequences of 8–9
 first 19–20, 54, 98, 182–3,
  185, 189
 and the first sign of a
  problem **66**, 67–8,
  70, **78**
 frightening nature of 5
 and generalised anxiety
  disorder 17
 and goal-setting 42–5, 53
 and images 103–5, 211, *211*
 impact 25
 isolated 18
 limitations of living with
  201–2
 maintaining factors 25,
  66–81, **66**, 159
 making sense of 19–20
 night-time 50–1, 59–60
 'normal' 6
 and panic cycles 82
 and panic diaries 85, *86–7*,
  88, *208–9*
 personal accounts of 8
 and phobias 17
 and post-traumatic stress
  disorder 16–17
 prevalence 5
 and recovery stories 26,
  180–8, 189–95
 recurrent 83–4
 and relapse management
  26, 159–63, 165–7,
  169, 171–2, 174, 177
 role in panic disorder 6,
  15–16, 19
 and safety behaviours 75,
  76–7, 77, **78**, 79, *207*
 and sanity 9, 11, 62, *65*, 68
 severity level *86–7*, 96,
  199
 and the situation **66**, 67–8,
  70, 71, **78**, *86–7*

and social anxiety disorder 16
strategies to overcome 91, 92–103, 105–7, 109, *110*, 111–33, *116–17*, *121*, 136–7, 142–4, 148, 153–4, 156–7, 211
symptoms of 5, 8–9
and thinking something bad will happen 105–7
and thoughts 9, **66**, 67–9, 70, 71–3, 80–1
triggers of 58, 59, 64–5, 68–9, 71
types of 58–9
and understanding the nature of anxiety 108–9, *110*
and understanding the role of thoughts and images in 103–5, *211*
unpredictable nature of 13–14, 15, 52, 55, 58–9, 64, 106
waking up to 84
and the weekly review form *210*
and wellbeing reviews *230–1*
what happens during? 58–62, **63**
see also case examples
panic cycles 25, 58, 68–72, 74, 78–82, **78**, 85, 88
and making notes 31
and recovery stories 187, 188, 191
and the relapse management toolkit 160, 164
strategies for overcoming 90, 95, 98, 112, 117, 132
worksheet **206**

panic diaries 85, *86–7*, 88, 185
and strategies for overcoming panic disorder 90–1, 95–8, 101, 132, 156
worksheet *208–9*
panic disorder 1–46
agoraphobia as complication of 6, 10–11, 13, 19, 24–5, 39, 54–6, 64, 74, 80–2, 144–7, 164, 189–95
case examples 23, 49–58
causes of 18–20
and CBT 20
definition 6
diagnosis 7–8, 184
difference from other anxiety disorders 15–18
early warning signs 84
fear of the panic attacks of 13–14
and the *fight or flight* response 60–1
and gender bias 6
and goal-setting 32–3, 41–6, 53, 57
improvement in 169–72, 174, 180, *228–9*
life-limiting nature 14, *201–2*
medication for 15, 34–5
overcoming 81–4
preparing to tackle 85
prevalence 6
psychological cage of 14
recovery stories 26, 181–95
recurrent 83–4
symptoms 7–8, 9–10, 170, 193–4, *198*
understanding 4–22, 24–5, 47–88
workbook 27, 197–232

see also CBT self-help; relapse management toolkit; strategies to overcome panic disorder
panic disorder symptom scale (PDSS) 9–10, 93, 95, 101–2, 156, **199**
phobias 17
  blood/injury 120, 122
  see also agoraphobia
pink rabbit experiment 103–5, 191, *211*
post-traumatic stress disorder (PTSD) 16–17
procrastination 36
progress 169–72, 174, 180, *228–9*
public transport, fear of using 6, 11, 12, 31–2, 54, 74, 170, 194–5, *200*

recovery stories 26, 181–95
'red flags' 164, 166–9, 172–3, 176, 178, 187, 193, 193–4, 194, *227*
reflective practice 72, 117, 152, 169–70, 171
  weekly review form 101–2, *210*
relapse management toolkit 25–6, 83, 159–80, 188
  and early warning signs 164, 166, 166–9, 167–9, 172–3, 176, 178
  and identifying other areas you would like to work on 174–6
  and issues for the future 175–6, *232*
  and reflective practice 169–70, 171
  top tips 176–7
  and wellbeing reviews 173–4, 177, 193–5, *230–1*

relationships 169, 170

safety behaviours 69, 72, 73–9, **78**, 90, **91**
  and panic attacks 75, 76–7, 77, **78**, 79
  and recovery stories 186, 188
  and relapse management 163–6, 168, 172
  and strategies to overcome panic disorder 98, 99, 100, **100**, 122, 124–5, 132–7, **133**, 144, 146, 149, 151, 156
  worksheet **207**
  see also avoidance behaviours; escape behaviours
self-compassion 164
self-criticism 177
setbacks 25–6, 32
  as learning opportunities 153
  and relapse prevention 160, 162–3, 165, 167, 177
sex 55, 57, 59, 75, 190–1, 195
situations **66**, 67–8, **70**, 71, **78**, 86–7
  see also dangerous situations
social anxiety disorder 16
social lives 169, 170
social pressures 35
strategies to overcome panic disorder 25, 89–157, 90–2, *91*, 96–7, *101*, 133–52
  discovery experiments 90, *91*, 92, 95–6, 101, 102–32, 148–9, 153–5, 185, 188, 191, *211–23*
  and relapse prevention 166–7, 175
  summing up 155–7

testing experiments 90–2,
    91, 96–7, 101, 133–56,
    133, 172, 185–6, 188,
    191–2, *224–5*
time management 94–7,
    155
troubleshooting 152–5
weekly reviews 101–2,
    210
stressful situations 18, 162
suicidal thoughts 38–9
support 21, 23, 28–9, 35–6,
    37–9, 81
    lack of 154
    and recovery stories 184
    and relapse prevention 159,
        161, 167, 175, 178–9
    and strategies to overcome
        panic disorder 94, 95,
        134, 143, 147–8
'symptoms contrast' (exercise)
    120
symptoms of panic disorder
    7–8, 9–10, 170, 193–4,
    198
    see also panic disorder
        symptom scale

testing experiments 90, 91, *91*,
    92, 96–7, 101, 133–56,
    133, 172
    for avoidance 144–9, *145*
    and diary-keeping 137,
        143–4, 148–9,
        224–5
    panic attacks during 154
    and predictions 92, 134,
        138, *140–1*, 142–3,
        146, 149–50, *224–5*
    and recovery stories 185–6,
        188, 191–2
    worksheets *224–5*
thoughts 48–9, 66, **91**
    catastrophic 65, *65*, 68

interpreting body
    sensations in a
    catastrophic way 19,
    56, 59, 64–5, *65*, 69,
    70, 71–3, 84, *86–7*, 90,
    92–3, 99–100, **100**,
    102–3, 105–9, *110*,
    111–34, *116–17*, **129**,
    148–9, 151, 154, 156,
    163, 165, 185, *211–23*
not listening to your 33
and panic attacks 9, 52,
    56, **66**, 67–73, **70**, **78**,
    103–5, 211, *211*
racing **63**, *65*
and relapse prevention 168
and safety behaviours 90
and strategies to overcome
    panic disorder 98–100,
    100
threat, feelings of heightened
    17
time management 36, 94–7,
    155
triggers of panic attacks 58, 59,
    64–5, 68–9, 71
    external 64, 67
    internal 64, 67
troubleshooting 152–5

unreality experiments 127–9,
    129

vicious cycles 68–72, 82, 90, **91**

wellbeing reviews 173–4, 177,
    193–5, *230–1*
women, and panic disorder 6
work life 169, 170, 189–90
workbook 27, 197–232